GET YOUR $HIT TOGETHER

GET YOUR

THE REBEL MAMA'S HANDBOOK FOR

$HIT

FINANCIALLY EMPOWERED MOMS

TOGETHER

ALEKSANDRA JASSEM
NIKITA STANLEY

Collins

Published by Collins, an imprint of HarperCollins Publishers Ltd

First edition

HarperCollins Publishers Ltd
Bay Adelaide Centre, East Tower
22 Adelaide Street West, 41st Floor
Toronto, Ontario, Canada
M5H 4E3

www.harpercollins.ca

Library and Archives Canada Cataloguing in Publication
Title: Get your shit together : the rebel mama's handbook for financially empowered moms / Aleksandra Jassem, Nikita Stanley.
Other titles: Rebel mama's handbook for financially empowered moms
Names: Jassem, Aleksandra, author. | Stanley, Nikita, author.
Description: The word "shit" appears as a dollar sign ("$") on source of information. | Includes bibliographical references.
Identifiers: Canadiana (print) 20200320718 | Canadiana (ebook) 20200320742 | ISBN 9781443461412 (softcover) | ISBN 9781443461429 (ebook)
Subjects: LCSH: Mothers—Finance, Personal—Handbooks, manuals, etc. | LCSH: Finance, Personal—Handbooks, manuals, etc. | LCSH: Budgets, Personal—Handbooks, manuals, etc. | LCGFT: Handbooks and manuals.
Classification: LCC HQ179 .J37 2020 | DDC 332.024—dc23

Printed and bound in the United States of America

LSC/C 9 8 7 6 5 4 3 2 1

To independence.

CONTENTS

Part 3: SPENDING

Part 4: DEBT

Part 5: SAVING

Part 6: INVESTING

PREFACE

It's 5:11 a.m. and you have to pee—again.

It's been like this for the past few mornings, and every night at 9:50 p.m., you've been falling into the deepest sleep of your life. Your boobs hurt. Your lower back aches. Your whole body feels swollen—like all the carbs you've eaten lately have finally caught up to you. You cried at work this Tuesday; you had a wicked hangover after two glasses of wine on Thursday. On Saturday it dawns on you: Your period is late.

You buy a pregnancy test and leave the untouched package on the counter for 24 hours while you continue to live your best non-impregnated life from Saturday evening to Sunday night. Finally, you muster the guts to pee on that stick and learn your fate.

You wait 30 minutes (the suggested 20 minutes plus 10 to be safe) and re-enter the bathroom.

You approach the vanity and catch your own eye in the mirror. One last glance at the woman who didn't know . . .

You're pregnant.

Holy fuck.

Suddenly the ground beneath you starts to give out. Your mind shoots in a million directions at once. Boy or girl? Twins or singleton? Will we have to move? *Can we actually afford this?*

You're excited, you're terrified, you're acutely aware of the financial ramifications of inviting a very small, very cute, very revenue-negative roommate into your heart and home for the foreseeable future.

With the affirmative pee stick still sitting on the bathroom counter, you make a vow to yourself and to your unborn child that you're going to grow up. You're going to be better. You're going to reel it in and stop spending money like an asshole—for their sake and for yours.

You exit the bathroom, tell your partner the happy news, and enjoy a private celebration. That night, you lie in bed, hand on belly, staring up at the ceiling, experiencing a full-blown existential/financial crisis. The next day, you enter research mode.

If this is where you are in your journey right now, then good on you, sister! (And congrats!) You took your curiosity and did exactly what you were supposed to do with it: You let it inspire you to learn.

From experience, however, we know that there's a good chance you've sought financial enlightenment a bit later in your mom career. You see, the initial glimmer of financial curiosity is often fleeting because sometime during a woman's second trimester, she enters *mama-bear mode:* a state of being wherein thoughts go from pragmatic to primitive. Steam-cleaning the curtains seems more urgent than looking into Registered Education Savings Plans (RESPs), and spending your life's savings on a Restoration Hardware nursery set and a $2,000 stroller sounds like a practical allocation of funds.

Yup. Been there, bought that.

Blame the hormones. Blame the algorithms. Blame the ads. But as your belly expands, your inner dialogue starts to chatter and all it says is "Focus on the baby. Nothing matters but the baby. Just keep doing things and acquiring things for the baby." So you go and you do and you acquire and it's *all* about the baby. You defer financial responsibilities to your partner (bad idea), and you hire someone to clean the house (great idea), so that you can attend classes about the baby and doctor's appointments about the baby. You register for the baby and celebrate the baby and then one day: You have the baby.

During the early days of new motherhood, it's legitimately *impossible* to give a shit about anything other than figuring out what exactly goes into keeping an infant alive. You learn to swaddle, master different shushing techniques, and attempt new modes of feeding. You become a human mattress and vomit receptacle. You change diapers full of mustard-yellow shit (theirs) and diapers full of crimson-red blood (yours). You align your rhythm with your baby's. You become one with them (again). You're enveloped in the baby haze. But then one day . . . clarity.

You emerge from the fog and step into a new realm of (mostly) uninterrupted sleep and small but valuable increments of alone time. It takes a few months to get there, but eventually the world that exists beyond the four corners of your baby's nursery comes back into focus. You can think again. Your priorities have shifted, though, and now the looming prospect of going back to work seems even more horrifying. The pull to stay home is real. You start to consider your options: going back to the career you left to have your baby; finding a new (more flexible) job that hopefully still constitutes a lateral career move; or extending your hiatus even longer—"at least until they're in school"—before eventually re-entering the workforce. You can sense that in making this decision, a significant amount of access is at stake: access to money, access to power, access to the conversations that matter.

For the past six years, we have used the Rebel Mama platform to give modern moms—notwithstanding their vocation—access to the conversations that affect them most. We've written blog posts and books to help moms step into their power and advocate for their mental and emotional well-being. For six years we smashed stigmas and dismantled taboos. For six years we've fostered community connections and built a modern village to support a new generation of child-bearers. For six years we busted our asses in the name of empowerment, and do you know what we learned in the process? We learned that for six years we'd been overlooking the most important piece of the empowerment puzzle: *Money.*

Money is the international language of power, which means that empowerment simply cannot be fully realized without financial literacy. The old adage "He who has the gold makes the rules" still holds true. The goal now is to amend the pronoun. In order to do that, you'll have to become financially literate first.

Financial literacy is what this little gold handbook has been designed to give you. It's everything that school didn't teach you about money—how to earn it, spend it, save it, invest it, and teach your kids about it. This is a girlfriends' guide to finance. A no-judgment, no-bullshit cheat sheet of all the things you need to get your $hit together when you've got a family to account for.

We've been at this mom gig for a while now, and what we know for sure is that moms need so much more than a day at the salon to take care of themselves. We don't need healing crystals or essential oils or a facelift for our vaginas, and we certainly don't need *another* suggestion to stock up on wine. What moms really need is someone to show them a clear-cut path to economic freedom. Fuck bubble baths—this is the real self-care.

Whether you're debt-ridden and broke or you have some money in the bank that you simply don't know what to do with, anytime is a good time to take control of your financial future. To do it, you'll need to do two simple things:

1. Learn the game.
2. Plan to win it.

Let us teach you the rules and help you with your plan, babe—Virgo-style (read: interactive pages and checklists galore). Come with us on this journey of learning, debunking, and understanding. Spoon with your pregnancy pillow, strap your baby to your boob, or settle in on the sidelines of your kid's soccer practice. No matter what stage you're in, listen up because we're doing this. We're entering the final frontier of empowerment together.

We can't afford not to.

GLOSSARY OF REBEL MAMA TERMS

Occasionally, we like to employ words/acronyms that don't technically exist in the English language. While some of their meanings are obvious, others may have you pausing to consult Google—and we certainly don't want that happening—so we've created a little glossary for you to familiarize yourself with before we begin.

AF: As fuck

ATM: At the moment

BFF: Best financial friend

BIWOC: Black/Indigenous/ women of colour

DGAF: Don't give a fuck

DIY: Do it yourself

GD: Goddamn

Hella: Extremely

IRL: In real life

JOMO: Joy of missing out

NBD: No big deal

OBV: Obviously

OG: Original gangster

PIC: Parent in charge

ROI: Return on investment

SAHM: Stay-at-home mom

THE PRICE OF MOTHERHOOD

"The truth will set you free, but first it will piss you off."—*Gloria Steinem*

Keep that in mind as you plough through the pages of this book—especially this chapter.

Remember, for better or for worse, understanding the odds as they're stacked against us is the key to winning the game. We have a responsibility to educate ourselves on exactly where we stand financially as mothers and women before we make our move on one of the world's most uneven playing fields.

Everyone knows we (women) pay the physical price of child-bearing with our bodies. Bone and muscle density decrease, teeth and gums weaken, skin stretches, and pelvic floors give out. But you're about to learn the true cost of being a woman/mother, and seeing the numbers on paper may be worse than slightly pissing your pants every time you sneeze.

So just how much is this whole "lady" gig going to cost you in dollars and cents?

Maggie McGrath of *Forbes* asked the same question a few years back and found that (brace yourself) based on a 40-year career, you're looking at about $40,000 USD—and that's only if you're white. The losses recorded among BIWOC are even more appalling. Sharing findings from the National Women's Law Center 2016 study of the wage gap, McGrath notes that Black women will earn $877,480 less than a male counterpart over a 40-year career, Indigenous women will earn $833,040 less, and Latinx women will earn a mind-blowing $1,007,080 less throughout their working life.

Okay, fine, but it can't be *as bad* in Canada, right?

Wrong.

In Canada, notwithstanding sector or education level, the wage gap persists. On average, Canadian women earn 72 cents for every dollar earned by men, and unfortunately not even our fancy degrees can save us. As of 2016, women with university degrees were making 10 to 30 percent less than their male peers, according to Brittany Lambert and Kate McInturff of Oxfam Canada and the Canadian Centre for Policy Alternatives.

That's some bullshit right there if we've ever heard it. But wait—that's not even taking procreation into account. For mothers, the situation is even more grim.

According to Wealthsimple (Canada's leading digital investment company), "Canadian census data from 2011 shows that on average, after a first child,

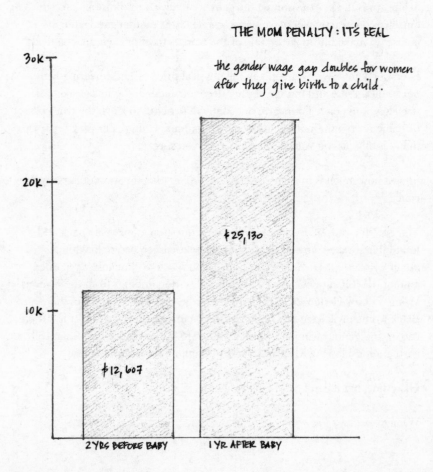

THE MOM PENALTY : IT'S REAL

the gender wage gap doubles for women after they give birth to a child.

$25,130

$12,607

2 YRS BEFORE BABY   1 YR AFTER BABY

a woman's earnings are 12 percent lower than that of childless women. That percentage grows with each additional kid, so that by the time a woman has her third or fourth she's earning 20 percent less." Great. Glad her expenses are skyrocketing at the same time. *deep eye roll*

Oh, and all of this has a name, by the way. It's the *Motherhood Penalty*, a term created by sociologists to describe the persistent pay gap between mothers and their child-free female associates.

Alright, so what's to blame here?

Is it that women and men tend to work in different occupations, and the occupations where women work usually come with lower wages? Or that globally, women spend between three and six hours every day on domestic and caregiving work (by comparison, men spend between 30 minutes and two hours on similar activities), thereby reducing hours that women can spend earning? How about the social science research that shows that moms are likely to be (erroneously) seen by employers as less competent and more apathetic about work than their child-free colleagues?

Of course, *all* these things (in addition to myriad other socio-political factors) are to blame. But solving the problem of gender inequity is not the goal of this book. The goal of this book is simply to encourage you to get interested in the game of money. We want you to ask yourself hard questions about the role you want to play in society and consider the effects that role will have on your financial well-being.

One thing we'd all be well served to contemplate: How is the level of gender inequity we're experiencing *still* happening even though in *every* developed country and at *every* level of the socio-economic scale women today are actually more educated (thus, more primed for future success) than men? Consider the following statistics compiled by Wealthsimple:

> In the US, in 2016, women earned 30 percent more bachelor's degrees, 45 percent more master's degrees, and 13 percent more PhDs than men. In Canada, in 2016, 40.7 percent of women had a bachelor's degree, compared with only 29.1 percent of men. Throughout Europe, an estimated 10 percent more women have graduated college than men.

This is a phenomenon that *should* translate to higher earnings over time, so what gives?

As it turns out, the answer to that question lies somewhere deep in our subconscious minds. In 2015, a prominent researcher named Marianne Bertrand published a paper showing that even when a woman has the potential to earn more than her husband, she is unlikely to do so. But that's not even her most rattling finding. Evidently, in a heterosexual relationship in which the wife outearns her husband by 50 percent or more, the woman is likely to quit her job or scale back on work within two years of holy matrimony. Horrified yet? Well, brace yourself because she also found that if a lofty earner doesn't scale back on the work front, she'll ramp up on the home front instead—taking on more housework to ensure heteronormative gender roles continue to reign supreme.

What. The. Actual. Fuck. How did the conscious mind become so disconnected from the subconscious mind? And why are we putting the latter in charge of the decision making?

Listen. We are all for you making choices for yourself and your family that make sense practically, personally, and financially—as long as you understand the nuances of your options and the ramifications of your decisions before you settle on a course of action.

Want to quit your job and be a stay-at-home mom? Power to you, sister—that shit is not easy, and it deserves a hell of a lot more respect than it typically receives. Want to get out of the rat race and create your own dream job that allows you the flexibility to be present for your kids? Yas queen. It's the road less travelled, but from experience we can tell you that it's incredibly rewarding. Want to defer parental leave to your husband ASAP so you can get back in the corporate saddle and dominate as you lactate? We support that decision fully and unequivocally. Just know that there are practical steps you can take to ensure you remain financially empowered no matter what path you choose.

Think of this book as a bird's-eye view of all the incredibly complex decisions you'll have to make about work and life (and the so-called balance of the two) when you're starting a family. We're here to show you how to prioritize your funds and how to work to create personal and generational wealth. And we're here to help you dodge all the consumer traps (and bad financial advisors) that'll pop up along the way.

Motherhood, after all, is intuitive—it really doesn't require much *stuff*—and self-care has little to do with the newest aromatherapy candles or an over-priced trip to the salon. True self-care comes in the form of financial freedom, and it's yours for the taking if you can get over the fear of screwing up/the desire to keep up appearances and start thinking like a boss.

We promise, once you set yourself up for financial freedom, you can drown in all the CBD bath bombs and crystal dildos you want—perhaps even with a side of Dom Pérignon if you fancy. But if you can't afford to pay it off before you start paying interest on it, you better put that credit card back in your wallet, sister, and step away from whatever online shopping cart is currently open in your browser.

And don't come at us with excuses and justifications on why you *need* that new frock.

You gotta be stronger than your impulsive desires to do this work.

This is a game of mental prowess.

(Luckily, you've got that in spades.)

Now, let's go get that money.

FIRST THINGS FIRST: GET YOUR MIND RIGHT

The only way to begin this journey to financial freedom is by looking at our current relationship with money. It's a loaded topic, but it's worth unpacking before you go opening that Tax-Free Savings Account (TFSA) and maximizing your Registered Retirement Savings Plan (RRSP) contributions. Now is the time to let go of everything you used to feel/know about money and start with a clean state.

If you're anything like us, your relationship with money has always erred on the side of complicated. It's been attached to your highest highs and deepest lows. You love it, you hate it. You feel awkward talking about it, but you love spending it.

We're here to encourage you to wipe the slate clean. Commit to putting an end to old patterns of thought that previously kept you out of the game: It's time to redefine, refocus, relearn. If you can get over your history and open yourself up to a new kind of relationship with your finances, the *actual* money will be in the bag.

So how about a quick game of psychology to get your mind right?

Grab a pen and finish these sentences.

Don't rush. Allow yourself a moment to think.

Money is:

_____

Money makes me feel:

_____

What I love about money is:

_____

What I hate about money is:

_____

For me, financial freedom looks like:

_____

Now take some more time to reflect on each of your responses, and look deeper into what they stem from, what has shaped your ideas around money, what your attitude toward it has been, and what your goals look like now.

In life, we have power over two things and two things only: our thoughts and our attitudes. Notice them. Turn up the volume on your inner dialogue. Acknowledge and let go of any fear or anxiety that comes up in your response to money. Pay attention to things that trigger you. They are what's holding you back from taking control of your financial future.

And anytime you feel overwhelmed, remind yourself of this one simple truth: Money is not real. It's just an imaginary thing that was created to designate value to commodities so old-timey folk could quantify their goods and services. Only now it has evolved into a smorgasbord of strategic plays. Yes, money holds value, but it's not _real_ and it's certainly not something you should feel intimidated by.

Motherhood is real. Pizza is real. Love is real. Money? Money is a game, and anyone can play. Even us. Even you.

We simply need to be strategic, focused, and practical. Financial freedom is a long game of strategy, patience, and perseverance; if we want in, we must start with a vision and a plan. We have to put our blinders on, forget about keeping up with the neighbours/the friends/the Kardashians, and keep the focus on ourselves and our vision of financial freedom. Then we must use that to inform every earning, spending, saving, and investing decision we make.

In other words, we need to _get our $hit together._

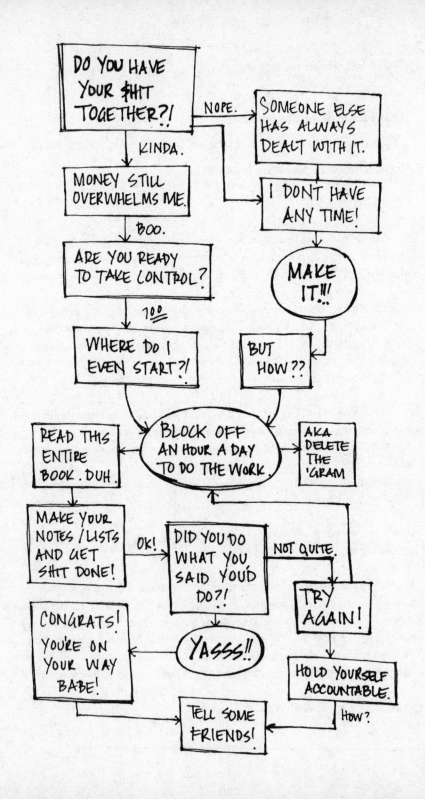

Part I

PLANNING

Planning for a baby is recommended because it allows you to make decisions about your future from a place of calm and logic. If they're left to the last minute, you run the risk of making hormonally charged, emotional decisions about serious shit like parental leave and living wills. Fear not, though. Our hand is extended, and we are ready to walk you through this process from beginning to end.

So, let's get to it, shall we?

HOW MUCH DO KIDS *ACTUALLY* COST?

Alright, bad news first: Kids cost a lot. Like, $270K a lot.

With figures like that, it's not hard to see why people are embracing a smaller family unit these days. Notwithstanding the number of kids you're hoping for, factoring monetary costs into family planning is important, as it provides excellent benchmarks for savings.

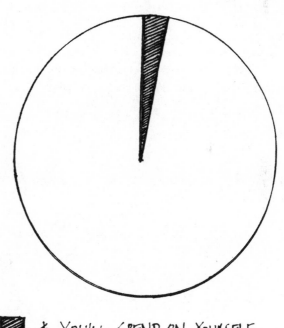

◼ $ YOU'LL SPEND ON YOURSELF

☐ $ YOU'LL SPEND ON YOUR SPAWN

(good times)

As mentioned above, in Canada, you're looking at an approximate lifetime spend of about $180–$270K (until the kid reaches the age of 18), and south of the border it's about the same. Although quarter-million-dollar figures can be intimidating, it's obviously much more manageable when broken down to monthly expenses (about $830–$1,250 per kid, per month). Of course, averages can be misleading because, as we know, one person's needs may be another's luxury.

Lucky for us, there's an easy way to calculate what the cost of raising a child would look like for you, specifically, because we live in the internet age and it's a blessing (for the most part).

Just hop on this website: www.themeasureofaplan.com/cost-of-raising-a-child-calculator. Then download the Excel or Google Doc file to get started on breaking down costs.

Knowing that a "bundle of joy" comes with one hell of a hefty price tag, it isn't hard to see why couples who choose to create human life together often also decide to amalgamate finances to help manage costs. But how does one do so sans drama? Read on, sister. We've got you covered.

JOINING FINANCES

*If you're raising kids solo, feel free to jump right into "Wills, Guardianship, and Other Morbid Thoughts" on page 17 (this is a fun book, we swear!).

It's becoming more and more common for couples to procreate out of wedlock. If you're married and you and your partner have already done all the "on paper" things like merging finances, then a lot of your work is behind you. If you and your lover are committed for the long haul, now would be a good time to give some thought to opening a joint account. Pooling all your cash for the sake of your child(ren) is your new reality. Woo-hoo! Let the good times roll.

Of course, as any therapist can quickly confirm, couples fight most about two things—sex and money—so if you're toying with the idea of dumping your funds together, you're going to have to go in eyes wide open and do it right. The obvious upside to all this is *financial transparency*. You will both have access to one another's data, so neither of you can be shady. This may or may not be the right move for you depending on your secret Amazon Prime life, but we're in favour of complete clarity to keep both parties accountable.

First, you gotta come clean about the skeletons in your closet. The student loans you're still paying off, your covert shoe fetish, and the not-so-impressive credit card debt you managed to rack up in Paris that one summer (among other things). By hiding your financial truth, you're missing out on some key components to a successful relationship—you know, like communication and honesty. Better to swallow your pride, air out all the dirty laundry, and get to work on a brighter future for the whole fam.

A quick note on income disparity: Chances are one of you will be outearning the other, which may leave one person feeling entitled and the other feeling like a pile of shit. The key in this scenario is adjusting your mindset to seeing your money as *combined income*: "Together we make *this*." Besides, we know all about that emotional labour (it's unpaid, remember?), so make sure to voice your grievances early to move forward in the right direction. This is about teamwork. This is about a partnership.

Together you can set goals, organize budgets, and live your financial lives to the fullest. A joint account literally doubles your economic potential and if you do it right, it will keep your relationship open, honest, and liberated AF.

That being said, you'll definitely want to allow for a little wiggle room in the old budget because scrutinizing every last penny and how it was spent ("Honey? Did you really just buy $60 face cream?") will dig a deep hole of resentment and kill all of the moods in your courtship. We recommend a separate savings account where a monthly value is set for "don't ask, don't tell" money. This could be $100 or $500 depending on your individual circumstance, and it could be allocated to anything from your vintage wine collection to the highlights you desperately need every spring. This way, you won't have to explain your damn self at every turn, and you'll have some flexibility to spend for pleasure . . . which is equally important.

Hot Tips for Tackling the Money Convo with Your Partner

- **Start the discussions early**—i.e., don't wait until there's an issue and emotions are running high.

- **Take baby steps** and get the easy stuff out of the way, like credit scores (more on those starting on page 129), before moving on to retirement planning.

- **Give your partner an idea of what's happening** in your life and your personal money goals. This can be anything from saving for a vacation to paying down debt to starting the business you've always dreamt of opening.

- **Create money goals together** and hold each other accountable— even if the goals start off small.

- **Talk about your respective upbringings.** Many of our opinions and attitudes toward money started in our childhoods at home.

- **Cite an article (any article) about money and marriage,** and see where the convo goes from there.

Structuring a Joint Account

So you've made the decision to join forces with another human being. Look at you! Adulting with your bad self. But what's the best approach? The truth is, there's a whole lotta ways you can make this deal work and each is unique to your personal needs and current circumstances. But for the sake of getting the wheels in your head spinning, here are some *Forbes* magazine–approved ways to combine and conquer:

Separate . . . but Together

This strategy entails keeping most of your money separate but contributing an equal set amount to one joint account to cover living expenses (think rent, utilities, groceries, cable). It's ideal for couples who may live together but don't need any messy commitments beyond that.

Earn More/Give More

In this scenario you will maintain separate accounts in addition to a joint account, except each person contributes a percentage of their income rather than a set amount to cover all essentials. This strategy works well for couples who experience notable income disparity but want to live a shared lifestyle. According to the experts at Wealthsimple, you want to be spending about 50 percent of your income on fixed household expenses (or "needs"), so keep that in mind as a contribution benchmark.

"I've Got This, Babe"

You guessed it: In this arrangement, Money Bags steps up and pays for all household expenses. It's an appropriate option when one person brings in substantially more than the other or when one partner is currently in school, staying home to raise babies, or otherwise not bringing in an income. The lesser-earner may cover some of the "fun" expenses, but for the most part, living expenses are covered by one party. Note: It's important (especially for unmarried cohabitants) to keep communication open around this arrangement (i.e., if you break up, will money be owed?) so it doesn't lead to conflict later.

Picky Pants

This option requires laying out all household bills and expenses and deciding together who will cover what. These may or may not add up to equal value. Bill picking is ideal for couples not earning the same incomes, or for partners who are not yet ready to officially amalgamate finances. It also works well if one person is living in a home that's owned by the other. Again, communication is key here as both parties have to agree. And if you want to be a total keener about it, draft up a casual but binding agreement (read: detailed email).

One Big Happy Bank Account

Combining all money in one pot, completely—a solid choice for couples who don't enter marriage with separate assets and want to share all the expenses from the get-go. Decide how you want to deal with any outstanding debts, discuss savings and any financial goals, and don't forget to leave a little room for "fun money" (either keep it in the one account or transfer it out to separate personal accounts). You need to enjoy a bit of it, too!

One Spends, One Saves

The idea here is that both partners are earning, but they live off one income and save the other. This makes sense when one party's income is inconsistent, or when the goal is to live on a single income in the future. Set up your budget to account for one income only and use it for everything. Funnel the second income straight into a savings or tax-sheltered investment account.

WILLS, GUARDIANSHIP, AND OTHER MORBID THOUGHTS

Remember when commercials didn't make you cry, and the news didn't make you shudder with fear? Yeah, well, that was pre-parenthood; now everything is emotional fair game. Tragedies happen, accidents occur, and shitty news is rampant every day on the six o'clock news. But now there's a child involved, and it all takes on a whole new meaning.

Mortality is not something anyone likes thinking about, much less discussing, but death is part of life and it's one thing you have very little control over. You do, however, have control over what happens after you bite the dust, and you'd be nuts not to plan for it.

Having a living will is arguably one of the most important things you can do as a parent, and although it isn't as much fun as putting together your modern minimalist registry, it's much more necessary. We're guessing you'd like your children to be provided and cared for exactly as you wish in the (unlikely, but still possible) event that both parents should suddenly die. And if you happen to live a long and beautiful life, you will have had peace of mind when you travelled, left your children with others, and generally gone through life unscathed. If you don't take the lead and allocate assets, finances, guardianship, and all that yourself, guess who will? The government. And do you really want them making decisions about your estate on your behalf? We didn't think so.

The good news is, you don't necessarily need a lawyer to draft up a will, and these days it's easier than ever to hop online and start the process yourself from the comfort of your home. But because we know this is one of those things that you'll easily put off, we've enlisted some help from Wealthsimple to put together this questionnaire to get the ball rolling and make this grim reaper process a little less daunting.

Who will my executor be?

An executor is someone you'll appoint to carry out the instructions of your will. It's important to choose someone who knows you very well so your voice can be heard, but also someone who is calm, resolute, organized, and trusted by those in the will. Note: Keep executors in mind when compensating in said will—they obviously deserve a slice of the pie.

Who will I appoint to be the legal guardian of my children?

Consider where you want your children (18 years and younger) to be raised, who your values align with most, and who will work best with your executor—the two will be making some hefty decisions together, so you want to make sure the vibe is positive.

What charities, if any, would I like to give to?

This is not as simple as "give all my money to cancer research" and will require a little more thought. Do the research and make sure your donation reaches the cause you want to help. Also, do your tax research as you can gain advantages for beneficiaries if you plan right.

Who gets what?

Ah, the pending questions of who gets your autographed Michelle Obama book and the heirloom ring gifted to you by your favourite aunt. But it's not just about the value of said objects; it's also about meaning. This is where you can thoughtfully leave something behind as a loving memory your close ones can cherish after you're gone.

Can I afford to draft a will?

The cost will vary depending on complexities, but typically it'll run you about $700 to $1,000 to do it right. Or get down quick and dirty with online services that'll run you around $100 and get the basics covered.

So now we will pose a follow-up question to the last one: Can you afford not to?

LIFE INSURANCE (YAWN)

Although some of the commercials are award worthy and funny as hell, the topic of life insurance itself is slightly depressing and mostly boring AF. We urge you, however, to give it a ponder as it's actually a very necessary duty—especially when you have a family. You don't really want to leave the people you love high and dry, do you? Of course you don't. So, although it involves exactly *zero* glamour, this shit is really fucking important, so just do it already.

Now, let's quickly get a few life insurance details ironed out with some help from our pals from Wealthsimple so we can move on to more exciting things, shall we?

Why You Need Life Insurance

In case you die sooner than expected (of course, you have no way of knowing), your immediate family will be liable for any outstanding loans, debts, mortgage payments, and all that other fun stuff. If you have a spouse or children who depend on you financially, life insurance is a no-brainer. You want to rest assured that even if your savings weren't up to par, your fam will be able to cash in on *something*. At the very least, they will be able to cover funeral arrangements. (Death doesn't have to be sad *and* expensive, does it?)

Coverage and All That Jazz

Typically, you'll be signing up for Term Life Insurance, which means you'll be paying a fixed annual premium for a certain number of years (usually 10, 20, or 30). If you die during that period, the insurance company will pay a predetermined amount of money to the beneficiary, and if you don't die (awesome news!), the insurance company keeps the cash and you never see it again (not so awesome, but such is life). Nevertheless, it still makes sense to buy it when you need it most (a.k.a. your prime working years) for a relatively low cost.

Other Policy Options

If you're fully loaded and have more savings than you could spend in a lifetime (bless), you can also look into Permanent Insurance, which provides lifelong protection and a massive payout, but this is a very expensive option to contribute toward, so unless you're MacKenzie Bezos, move right along.

Getting the Best Deal

There is no best deal. Whether you scour the internet for days, meet up with a slew of referred brokers, or pay a visit to the same guy who hooked your parents up 30 years ago, chances are you will end up with the same options from the same group of large insurers, for relatively the same price. The insurance industry is highly competitive and very well regulated, giving you the advantage to basically buy from whomever you like. (Here's where you get to choose whose commercial spot you enjoyed the most in the playoffs.)

Naming Your Beneficiary

Your spouse, your kids (if they are over 18), or a loved one you trust are all solid options. In regard to children under the age of 18, insurers are not legally allowed to pay out to minors, so if you want the cash in their hands and their hands only, you can set up a Life Insurance Trust, name that trust the beneficiary, and then appoint a family member as the trustee to carry out your wishes.

How Much and How Long

To get an idea of a number that's somewhat accurate (most insurance companies will have a handy calculator online to aid in the process), calculate all the expenses that your family would need to cover and make sure to include outstanding debts and non-monetary contributions—i.e., if you are currently the main caregiver to your children, factor in childcare. In terms of longevity, it's best to cover yourself until your mortgage and children's education is paid off; after that, it just depends on your personal goals.

The Importance of Medical Health

Not gonna lie, it'll obviously make a difference to an insurer whether you hack butts all day or not. Be prepared to answer a long list of health questions online or on the phone, including questions about your family's medical history to determine your risk. (Note: Many large insurance companies in Canada have updated their policies and moved marijuana use out of the high-risk category—where tobacco use currently resides. Least there's that!)

Low Budget Is Still Better Than No Budget

Something is better than nothing, so opt for a smaller, less expensive option to ensure your family gets *some* help if you can't afford all the snazzy add-ons. Always better than no help at all.

Hot Guy Break!

Just making sure you're not falling asleep, babe! Let's get that energy level back up.

SHIT YOU'LL WANT TO REMEMBER TO APPLY FOR ONLINE ASAP

Long-Form Birth Certificate

The holy grail of "primary documents." You'll need this in order to apply for most things pertaining to your kid, including everything listed below and baby's first passport (which we also suggest getting sooner rather than later. We brought our kids in to get theirs at 10 weeks old). Of course, you'll have to wait until the baby is here to apply, but it's something that can be done in the first days of being home or even in the hospital bed if you're feeling ambitious and have a good connection to Wi-Fi.

Social Insurance Number (for the Baby)

Yes, this is the number that allows your kid to get a job. We are not advocating for infant labour (though if your child should get a lucrative commercial contract modelling baby shampoo, it wouldn't hurt), but you'll also need that number to open up a Registered Education Savings Plan (RESP)—more on that later.

Health Card

You'll want to get that baby all the health care services it needs and since the government (a.k.a. your tax) covers it in most provinces in Canada, you'll want to settle that pronto. Make sure you read the specifics of what the program in your province covers, though, 'cause shit like dental and antibiotics comes straight out of your pocket, unless your work's health insurance plan covers it. If you need more coverage (or are in the US), private insurance/healthcare may be an option worth looking into.

Canada Child Benefit (CCB)

Formerly the Universal Child Care Benefit, the CCB is free fucking money from the government paid monthly to eligible families to help them with the cost of raising children under age 18. The amount of this benefit is calculated using the information you provide on your income tax returns. Parents get up to $6,400 per year for each child under the age of 6, and up to $5,400 per year for each child between the ages of 6 and 17. Don't assume you are ineligible because your family income seems too high. The eligibility calculations can be complex, and you might be missing a detail that qualifies you. Apply regardless and see what the CRA comes up with.

Daycare

We're not joking. The demand is high, the supply is low, and you might be on the wait-lists for up to a year, so get a head start and begin your search now.

BUDGETING (PHASE ONE)

Before you get started on anything else, you're going to need to prepare a very simple (and honest) budget to get you through the initial years of life as a parent. You need to understand what your money actually looks like on paper, familiarize yourself with your current financial habits, and plan for a future with more dependents and (temporarily) less cash flow. It's not as daunting as it sounds, and we promise you will feel a thousand times better once everything has been accounted for and organized.

We prefer throwing everything into Google Sheets (available to anyone with a Gmail account) for optimal organizational and updating capabilities, but, for now, jot it down here so you have no excuse to procrastinate.

First, figure out *what comes in* every month—in other words, calculate your **net income** (the money left over after taxes). If you're an entrepreneur, you will need to figure out a monthly average to work from. Gather your invoices for the year, add 'em up, divide by 12, and BAM—you have a monthly income average. Factor in year-end taxes here as well as any dividend or investment income.

Now for the less appealing part: You'll need to figure out *what goes out* every month—a.k.a. your **fixed expenses**. Make a list of all your monthly bills: rent, mortgage, water, electricity, car payments, gas, phone bill, health insurance, gym membership, Netflix/cable subscriptions, music subscriptions, credit card payments, and anything else that you pay monthly.

Doing this simple exercise will help you get in tune with your financial reality and show you places where you can easily save. Get into a habit of updating this sheet on a regular basis, and you will start to really feel in control.

Monthly Income (Cash Flying In)		Monthly Expenses (Cash Flying Out)		Leftover Cash (Income Minus Expenses)
Net Income One		Childcare		
Net Income Two		Extracurricular Activities		
		Banking Fees		
		Credit Card Payment		
		Mortgage Payment		
		Loan Interest		
		Contributions (RSPs etc.)		
		Car Payment		
		Heating/Cooling		
		Water		
		City Bills		
		Taxes		
		Groceries		
		Gas		
		Entertainment		
Total	$	Total	$	$

If you're doing this exercise pre-baby, now is a good time to ask yourself:

- Can your home accommodate your new family? Or will you have to move?

- Will you need to relocate to be closer to certain schools?

- Will you need to purchase a car or upgrade to something better/safer?

- How will you handle childcare?

- Will you buy clothes and toys second-hand? Or will you buy new?

- Will you start a college fund/RESP for your child(ren)?

- Will you start a savings fund for them?

- What will your incoming cash flow look like on parental leave?

Keep in mind that for baby's first year alone, you're looking at spending around $10K on average (this is why people have baby showers), but you can figure out what that would look like for you more specifically by using resources online—just google "baby cost calculator" and Bob's your uncle.

Fun times, hey?!

Baby's First-Year Expenses

Childbirth Expenses

Unless you want to upgrade to a private room, in Canada your hospital stay is on the proverbial house, but there may be extra costs for prescription drugs, as well as a doula or a midwife if you go that route.

Legal Expenses

If you don't yet have a will, this is the time to make that move, and to budget for it. As previously noted, a will can be drafted via the internet for relatively little, and inside a lawyer's office for a lot more (see page 17 for a refresher). And, of course, adoptive parents should factor in the legal expenses of that process, too.

Insurance Expenses

Life insurance may already be included in your job's benefit package (definitely worth a call to HR to be sure), but even if it is, you may decide to purchase more (again, refresher starting on page 19).

Baby Stuff Expenses

Don't worry, babe; it's actually not as bad as you think. Cribs, car seats, high chairs, etc., tend to be bought (or better yet gifted) once and passed down sibling to sibling, and they don't have to be top of the line (or even new) to complement the highly curated nursery you designed. Also, so much baby stuff is simply unnecessary (google "small house parenting" for proof). Do not get duped into thinking you *need* a wipe warmer, or a top-of-the-line baby monitor that measures baby's breathing, in order to be a good parent. We're here to tell you: You don't. There are, however, some other things you may not have thought of that you might decide you want: a CPR course ($150), someone to help you sleep train ($500+), and a breast pump plus accessories (call it $300). All that considered, you may want to give yourself a little cushion for unforeseen expenses (or hint to your mother-in-law that there are some practical items that you would likely get a lot of use out of especially in comparison to, say, a set of custom frilly crib sheets that cost $300?).

Sanity Preservation Expenses

If you can afford it, dedicate a little slice of the old budget to numero uno. Your kid and your partner (and you!) will be glad you did. Budget in some yoga classes, some new clothes that fit your new body—whatever it takes to make you feel a little bit like yourself again. And do not feel guilty factoring this stuff in. As long as you're not going into debt to pay for it, the ROI outweighs the cost.

Once you've got your fixed expenses figured out, time to list those **variable expenses**—a.k.a. fun expenses! But it's not time to throw a party just yet. Here you will be listing an average you spend on clothes, dinners out, food delivery, Ubers, happy hour drinks, overpriced candles, grocery store trips, Sephora trips, blowouts, facials, vacations . . . all that good stuff. Note: Your variable expenses will likely go down in your first year as a parent due to things like less extravagant vacations and limited bar hopping, so there is *some* solace.

Factor in everything, and you should walk out with a pretty good idea of what kind of lifestyle you'll be able to maintain avec bébé, and whether you'd like to expand the brood.

Remember, being completely reckless (*Fuck it! Let's have three more babies! We'll figure it out!*) feels a lot shittier when you can't feed your kids. Consider what you'd like to be able to spend on household help as well (childcare costs broken down starting on page 107) because that shit ain't cheap, so you'll want to plan.

Now it's time for some math.

Add up everything from the "expenses" column. Then add up everything from the "income" column. If your expenses are higher than your income or if you're just barely breaking even, unable to save a dime, it may be time to adjust some of those fun things that you clearly have no business doing. We know. *Buzzkill.*

Good news, though: Now you know what you're dealing with and you can properly plan, save, and take control of your financial health. Just don't forget to factor in the temporary financial roadblock that is parental leave (more on that starting on page 42).

WHAT ABOUT LONE PARENTS?

There is a growing population of brave heroes who are undertaking the challenge of raising kids solo. As of 2014, there were 698,000 single-parent households in Canada—that's 20 percent of families with kids under 16 (not far off from the 2017 global median of 24 percent). Out of those Canadian families, 81 percent are lone mothers; 78 percent of working lone mothers are employed full-time.

Let the record show that being employed full-time while simultaneously being solely responsible for the survival of small children is some next-level hard shit. It's a grind, a hard-won battle, but know that if this is your path, all the glory will be yours and yours alone in the end; remember to bask in that shit when the day finally arrives. In the meantime, you'll have to woman up and make some calculated decisions to ensure your family's financial well-being. That means building a rock-solid support system for yourself and your kid(s), accepting the financial assistance you qualify for, and ensuring that you're saving strategically for your family's future.

So, what kind of financial support is available?

Well, the first kind is **child support** and it's due from the guy with whom your child shares DNA. The guiding principle of Canada's child support laws is that children of intact families benefit from both parents' incomes and that should not change if their parents separate or divorce. Child support should be paid monthly and is calculated based on your ex's gross annual income and the number of kids you have together. While you definitely want to seek the help of a lawyer or mediator in sorting out the details, you can get an idea of what your monthly payout should be by using the Justice Department of Canada's Child Support calculator, which you can access online by googling it (#thefutureisnow). For reference, if your ex makes the 2018 average (male) annual income of $65,800 and you have two children together, you would be owed approximately $1,000 per month in child support.

By contrast to the male average, the average monthly income earned by a solo mom in Canada is only $3,237 or $38,874 annually (is it any wonder we're still yelling "Fuck the Patriarchy"?). In most provinces in Canada, this will land you right smack in the middle of the "low income" bracket. While that may be a blow to the old ego at first, it certainly bodes well for qualifying for government support or grants—things that were literally designed to make our country a more equitable place for everyone by giving us the financial boost we need when we need it the most (it's basically the reason Canada is considered one of the best countries in the world to live in). Use. That. Shit.

There is one main federal support channel here: The **Canada Child Benefit (CCB)**, formerly the Universal Child Care Benefit, which, if you followed the instructions starting on page 23, you've already applied for (right?). If you're a lone parent making approximately $40,000 a year, from this program alone you'll increase your annual income by approximately $5,000. You'll want to apply for it in addition to any other supplementary benefits offered by your province (in Ontario, for example, you may be eligible for the Ontario Child Benefit or the Ontario sales tax credit, which can offer up to $1,500 and $720 a year respectively), and you'll want to do so pretty much as soon as you give birth.

For lone parents, anything causing a temporarily diminished amount of earnings can have really damaging effects on the financial well-being of your family. If the worst-case scenario ever befalls you, here's what your safety net looks like in Canada:

Employment Insurance Family Supplement

The **Family Supplement** is an Employment Insurance (EI) feature that provides additional benefits to low-income families with children when a caregiver loses their job. The maximum Family Supplement is 80 percent of your average insurable earnings up to $25,921.

If your family receives the Canada Child Benefit, then you are eligible to receive the supplement on qualifying income levels. If you are eligible, the Family Supplement will automatically be added to your EI benefit.

Child Rearing Provision

Check your paycheques or call your workplace's HR department and confirm whether you've been contributing to the Canada Pension Plan (CPP). The CPP provides basic benefits to contributors who retire or become disabled. The benefit is determined by how long and how much you have contributed to the plan, so if you leave the workforce for a period, this is likely to lower your benefit in the future. The **Child Rearing Dropout provision** (CRDO), a.k.a. the Child Rearing provision, is a program offered by the CPP that you should apply for if your reason for leaving the workforce is to take care of children. You're going to want to get the highest possible payment when you finally do retire and the CRDO provision will make it happen. Without it, periods of low earnings would reduce your pension, but with the CPP applied, those years simply won't count when it comes time to calculate your benefit. South Beach, here you come, baby!

What about lone parents in the US? Don't worry; there is support available there, too.

Americans may qualify for tax breaks like the **Earned Income Tax Credit** (a benefit for working people with low to moderate income) or the **Child Tax Credit**, which gives you a tax break of up to $2,000 for each child living with you. Take note that if you owe less than the credit amount, you can actually receive up to $1,400 of the balance as a refund. This is known as the **Additional Child Tax Credit**.

Of course, not all lone parents need financial support from the government—there are women out there who are funding their families solo like it ain't no thing. But it's still good to know that there is a safety net available to you should you ever need it.

A SMALL VICTORY: (UNCOUPLING)

By Dr. Andrea Gelinas

Money and divorce—you want to talk about taboo topics for women? Those two top the list. But trust me, when it comes to finances and relationships, keeping yourself in the dark will inevitably come back around to bite you right in the ass.

In the last three years I opened my dental clinic, got pregnant with my son, and got divorced. I thought I was going to literally lose everything I'd worked so hard to build. I also thought I would never be able to handle the finances on my own.

But you know what saved me from that dreaded fate? Me.

For as long as I can remember, I was privy to my parents' conversations about finance. While the concepts were often too abstract for my young mind to fully unpack, being present for those discussions around the kitchen table at an early age gave me the ability to talk about money openly. I discovered that frankness is the cornerstone of constructive finance dialogue. That's the thing about money—it's really all about the numbers. We tie so much emotion into quite rational and logical concepts. Shame and embarrassment especially need not be involved.

For me, it was important to take the reins on the financial discussions in my (now dissolved) marriage and thank God I did. The honeymoon phase always seems idyllic. It's easy to look past all the things that will ultimately end up annoying the fuck out of you. But it clouds some of the important and difficult conversations you should be having—conversations about money.

I led those conversations because I had to. My ex is terrible with money. As a result, monthly budgeting became my best friend throughout our marriage. You hear about budgeting time and time again because it works. It lets you be transparent with yourself (and your partner, if applicable) about values and priorities. Think daily coffees and seasonal shoe purchases vs. the annual vacation. The simple act of budgeting allowed me to pay off all his debt (more on that later), and it allowed us to get ahead well before I thought that we could.

Then a culmination of factors resulted in our decision to permanently separate, and even though I had been the financial authority in our little family for a decade, I still felt an enormous amount of fear and anxiety about having to do it all—working, child rearing, financial planning—completely on my own. But here's where those early conversations and basic budgeting skills came in very handy. So handy, in fact, that they're the very tools that propelled me into the role of the heroine of my own story.

When my ex moved out, I got to work.

I knew exactly what my monthly expenses were and I forced myself to stick to my budget. I streamlined my groceries and ordered meal kits. I shopped around and cut my internet/cable/phone bill in *half*. I made more conscious decisions about my purchases. I'm not suggesting it's easy. These things are hard, but now I can see my hard-ass work finally paying off and, damn, that's liberating!

Ladies, my advice to you is as follows:

- **Take the emotions out of the equation:** You won't get anything accomplished while they cloud valuable headspace, and you certainly won't get ahead if you're too embarrassed to have the right conversations.

- **Ask for help:** If finances aren't your forte, ask someone to help you. Aside from reading, it's the only way to learn.

- **Surround yourself with an absolute dream team:** Put your financial advisor, accountant, lawyer, and bank manager on speed dial. Remember, they know a ton, including how to get creative, and ultimately they want you to succeed. If/when shit hits the fan, they will help you!

- **Create and follow your budget, and review it monthly:** Make it a priority—like a nerdy date night.

- **Contribute to everything you can:** RRSPs, RESPs, TFSAs. Regardless if it's $50 or $500, that shit adds up and can be a great tax break (you'll learn all about that starting on page 172). As you advance in your career, make more space for these contributions in your monthly budget. And if/when you get a bonus or raise, throw a chunk into these savings.

- **Always speak to a lawyer:** Do this before you make any big decisions like paying off your partner's debt or getting financial help from a family member—this could impact you in a divorce.

- **Allow yourself to be vulnerable:** Financial transparency is a must; then you can come up with a plan.

Befriend your budget, save often, and let logic rule, so that if—God forbid—you find yourself having to navigate these waters yourself, you'll be able to swim bravely to shore with intentional strokes.

Trust me, you can do this.

Part 2

EARNING

Earning is a fantastic way to get money into your bank account. Of course, having children makes earning slightly more complicated, since keeping kids alive and engaged is literally a full-time job in itself, but trust us when we tell you there are ways around those tiny (massive?) obstacles if you're open to finding them.

But wait . . .

HOW DO YOU FEEL ABOUT GOING BACK TO WORK AFTER BABY?

Have you busted your ass for your education? Are you exhilarated by your career?

Do you want to re-evaluate everything and choose a different career path altogether?

Does that career path require fresh schooling and certificates?

Are you over it all and ready to fully embrace being a full-time caretaker?

(At least until the kid(s) go to school?)

These are important life decisions, especially insofar as your financial future is concerned. So, let's ensure you know what your options are before you take a leap and choose your adventure.

Take the Quiz

Circle Y for "yes" or N for "no"

1. Will you return to your old job? **Y / N**

2. Will you find a new job to return to, with a different employer? **Y / N**

3. Will you work part-time? **Y / N**

4. Will you start your own business? **Y / N**

5. Will you go back to school to earn a new degree or certificate to further your career? **Y / N**

6. Will you put your career on hold to care for your kids full-time? **Y / N**

7. Will you re-enter the workforce after a four-year hiatus in a completely different capacity? **Y / N**

There. Now at least you have an idea of what you want.

If you answered yes to questions one or two and you make more than Canada's median income of $65K annually, consider yourself a **Bo$$**.

If you answered yes to questions two, three, four, or six and you make less than Canada's median income of $65K annually, you're a **Hu$tler**.

If you answered yes to question five, you're a **$cholar**.

If you answered yes to question six and are revenue negative or close to it, you're a **$AHM**.

If you answered yes to question seven, you are likely to experience all the categories at some point between giving birth and sending your kids off to school. Lucky you?

Let's take a closer look at how each of those play out IRL.

THE BO$$

Pros	Cons
A good job with a great salary	Long AF hours
Fulfillment on every level	Exhaustion on every level
Appreciating time with kids the most	Seeing kids the least
Bringing in $5,000 per month	Spending exactly half of it on childcare and housekeeping alone
Impacting workplace culture by setting new precedents	Facing biases in the workplace regardless
Being able to afford to outsource annoying household shit (like laundry)	Paying everyone. For everything. Always.
Having a nanny who cooks and cleans	Employing said nanny until the kids go to college
Financial independence	Major dependence on lists, schedules, and the army of people who keep the house running

Hot Tips for Bo$$es

- Equitably share parental leave with your partner (if there is one in the picture).

- If your partner goes back to work, too, get a nanny. That way you won't be calling in sick every time your kid catches a bug and needs a day on the couch to recover (although you will prob take the day to be with them if you can).

- If you don't have a partner, definitely get a nanny.

- If you don't want a nanny, get on daycare lists as soon as humanly possible (like, while your baby is still in utero).

- Make sure you've set yourself up for a triumphant parental leave return by following the advice below.

- Communicate with your partner if the housework scales become imbalanced—as you know, it's common for working women, even if they're family breadwinners, to take on more than their fair share of housework, and you'll want to avoid that distraction at all costs so you can focus on your kids when you're home.

- Budget for childcare for the next decade at least. Unfortunately, school ends three hours before your workday does (good times, right?), so after-care and before-care costs will follow you indefinitely.

- If you get back to work and decide you now really hate your job and life's too short to continue your current career path, apply to new companies whose values align with yours. If you're looking for flexibility, look for more remote-working options and try to negotiate for pay that's equal to what you left (P.S. you don't have to disclose your previous salary when you apply).

- On that note, if you're getting hired for a new job, you *do not* have to disclose the fact that you have children. In fact, your potential employer shouldn't be asking because if you don't get the job, you can point to the fact that they asked you about your family as evidence of discrimination on the basis of the protected ground of family status.

- If your new priorities are making it difficult to tolerate the daily minutiae of working life, focus on parts of your job that fulfill you by delegating tasks that are beneath your pay grade.

Parental Leave

Parental leave is definitely not the paid vacation you once so ignorantly imagined it would be. Rather, it is the necessary time off granted to someone who's got a tiny baby at home to take care of, because it's legitimately the only thing they will be able to manage. The amount of time a parent gets to take off from work varies depending on the country they reside in.

In the US you are guaranteed exactly jack shit in paid parental leave (sorry). In the UK you're guaranteed six months. In Canada you're entitled to three different types of leave: **pregnancy leave** (unpaid leave lasting up to 17 weeks); **maternity leave** (paid leave lasting up to 15 weeks for birth mothers—this leave can start up to 12 weeks before birth); and **parental leave** (paid leave that can be shared by mom and dad). If you're a mother who took pregnancy leave, you're guaranteed up to 35 weeks of leave; mothers (and fathers) who did not take pregnancy leave are entitled to 37 weeks of parental leave.

In sum, Canadian mamas receive 15 weeks of maternity leave (available to mom only) plus 37 weeks of parental leave (which can be shared with dad), which equals 52 total weeks of leave at 55 percent of their salary. Parents can split the leave as they choose once the mother has taken 15 weeks of her designated maternity leave. Couples may also take parental leave at the same time, but they can't double up on the benefits. Only one cheque is allowed at a time per household.

The rules were changed in 2019 and now Canadian parents also have an option to take up to 18 months of leave. If you take that route, you'll get the same total benefit, but the money will be spread out over more time—15 weeks of maternity leave for mama at the 55 percent rate, and the next 61 weeks of parental leave for either parent at 33 percent.

It's good to be Canadian, eh?

So, where does this magical money even come from? Does the government simply replace your salary while you're at home getting barfed on and never sleeping? Not exactly. This cash flow comes to you from a fund you have likely been paying into for much of your working life: Employment Insurance.

Canadians who have been paying into EI during the 52 weeks leading up to giving birth receive 55 percent of their gross income, up to $573 per week. There are subsidies available for households with incomes of $25,000 or less.

Take note, though: In order to qualify to receive benefits, you need to have accumulated 600 hours of employment (that's 15 weeks of work at 40 hours per week) *during which you contributed to EI* in the 52 weeks before your baby arrives. (In Quebec, parents only need to have earned $2,000.) That caveat often spells "o-h-f-u-c-k" for freelancing Hu$tlers who quickly (but not quickly enough) realize they've never contributed a cent to EI since opening their business and now they're giving birth in 35 weeks.

If you're a freelancing female who's actively planning her own conception (you're a badass, aren't you?), our advice is to hold off on pulling the goalie until either (a) you're confident in your ability to save a sizable nest egg over a 40-week period (while pregnant) or (b) you've accrued the necessary hours to meet the threshold for collecting EI once the baby is born.

Insider tip: Qualifying for EI can be as simple as picking up a part-time gig at a reputable company with a robust employee insurance program for the duration of your pregnancy. You'll only make 55 percent of whatever your salary is there, but hey—better than nothing, right?

Please also keep in mind that if you start contributing to EI through your own small business payroll, that "opt-in" does not end once your first leave is over, and any future investment you make—whether you take a leave again or not—is non-refundable. For some mamas, it simply doesn't make sense to start paying in.

This is something that we strongly advise you take up with your accountant. There are other ways to survive (read: saving up and taking a shorter leave of absence, followed by working part-time hours starting while your babe is still wee), and there certainly ain't no shame in that game, especially if you can afford to pay for help to allow you to work in peace. But either way you're going to want to know your options so you can plan accordingly.

So, how does one even begin to prepare for the dreaded financial hit that is parental leave?

Well, you can start by trying to live off the income you'll make from EI. If you can drop your spending by 45 percent and not slip into a deep well of debt, take that as a positive sign. Don't forget to factor in taxes, too. Money collected during parental leave is still considered taxable income, so that benefit cheque might be even slimmer than you thought. Bummer, we know. Don't worry, though. Your income may be low, but your expenses are going to be even lower. No more "late for a meeting" Ubers, way less $14 cocktails, very few spur-of-the-moment weekend trips . . . Look at that—your tiny little ball and chain is already making you a better/more fiscally responsible human being. Go, baby!

So how to do get your hands on this "free money" (that you'll actually be working harder for than any other money you've ever made in your life)? If you're a Canadian living in Canada, simply go online, get on the Service Canada website, and search "apply for EI" (or QPIP in Quebec). Fill out the forms, send 'em in, and you're done. Easy peasy.

Except, since nothing to do with the government is ever *that* easy, there is some fine print involved in this agreement that you should be aware of:

- EI benefits can only be claimed within the year following your baby's birth.

- After you submit your application, there will be a two-week waiting period before you'll receive any funds (read: there will be *no money* coming in for those weeks).

- During the 15 weeks of maternity leave, you're prohibited from earning any money.

- Once maternity leave is over, however, and parental leave starts, the parent on leave is allowed to earn up to $50 per week, or 25 percent of their weekly EI benefit, whichever is higher. There's even a pilot plan that may allow some parents to hold on to more of their EI benefits even if they keep working.

Again, when in doubt, get in touch with Service Canada, call your job's HR department, or talk to an accountant you trust to figure out how to navigate all the acronyms and legal jargon. You don't want to mess around with this shit and wind up getting dinged on a technicality come tax time.

"Be an adult," they said. "It'll be fun!" they said.

10 Reasons Why Dad Should Definitely Take Parental Leave

Equality is often portrayed as a female issue, but it's not; it's a business and economic issue. That's why when both men and women take parental leave upon having a child, everyone wins. The amount of parental leave your partner takes has a profound impact—not just on your home life but eventually on your career. But the lack of a dad-only leave (like the one they have in Quebec, for example) means fathers—most often the higher earners in heterosexual couples—are less likely to take time off. We strongly suggest you and your partner work together to develop a plan that allows you both to take time off to care for and get to know the baby you made together. The benefits of doing so are plentiful, but here are some of our favourites:

1. He will have an opportunity to learn caregiving traits (like being nurturing, passionate, and empathetic), which happen to be very important leadership qualities.

2. He will do more housework. Need we say more?

3. He will be more likely to continue his involvement in childcare activities, such as feeding and diapering.

4. His early bonding time will lay a strong foundation upon which to build a lasting relationship with your kids.

5. He will help transform the perception that caregiving is a female responsibility. Jared Cline, in an article for Catalyst: Workplaces That Work for Women, writes that "72 percent of men said they would have taken a longer parental leave if they had seen co-workers do so."

6. His participation on the home front will allow you to return to work sooner, which may benefit your pay and chances for promotion, thereby keeping you in the leadership pipeline.

7. It could save you a lot of money in future family therapy bills. According to Jared Cline, one way to avoid behavioural problems in boys and psychological problems in girls is to make sure they get lots of quality time with their dads.

8. Dad can rest assured that his employer will survive without him. In fact, there's a good chance that his workplace's productivity won't be affected at all in his absence. That doesn't have anything to do with his value as an employee; it simply means that when anyone—man or woman—has to take time off work to raise a family, their colleagues step up and keep the ship afloat (as they should).

9. The message he sends by not taking parental leave is clear: Work matters more. We're not relationship experts, but we're pretty sure that's the kind of attitude that can land a man dangerously close to "only getting laid on special occasions" territory.

10. Still not enough for you? Well, how about economist Elly-Ann Johansson's findings that spousal parental leave has a profound effect on moms. In fact, her 2010 study proved that "each additional month that the father stays on parental leave increases mothers' earnings by 6.7 percent." Oh, snap.

Go get that money, honey. Clearly your man could use some diaper duty in his life anyway.

Knowing Your Rights When Talking to Your Employer About Your Parental Leave

Telling your boss that you are pregnant constitutes one of the most anxiety-inducing conversations of a woman's life. Will they laugh? Will they cry? Will you cry? Will they be disappointed? Will they be angry? Will they picture you doing the deed that got you in "the familial way" in the first place? *cue breakdown in bathroom stall* The truth is, the conversation may feel like the most awkward 20 minutes of your life, but we're here to encourage you to not let that scare you out of grabbing this golden opportunity by the balls and taking it for all it's worth.

Of course, the more knowledge you have of your rights under (Canadian) employment law, the more empowered you will be in this conversation. That's why we asked our friend Sarah Coderre Thompson—employment lawyer, badass, and mother of two—for the legal lowdown and hot tips on how to prepare before striding into that meeting room and sealing the fate of your future employment.

This is one of the very few times in your life in which you'll receive free legal advice so get your fucking highlighter out and listen up. Sarah says here's what you need to know:

1. **Tell your employer about your upcoming maternity leave as soon as you feel comfortable.** Problems can arise if an employer feels like their employee misled them or inconvenienced them by not telling them about their pregnancy sooner, so tell your employer ASAP. Although there is a risk that you could be sidelined from exciting work as soon as the employer knows you are pregnant, there is also the possibility that if you wait too long, you may make it difficult for your employer to plan for your maternity leave, and this can strain your employment relationship.

2. **Be clear in discussing what your rights are with your employer.** Most employment issues around maternity leave come up because an employer does not know what they are legally obligated to provide to their employees. In order to avoid some of these issues, you'll want to make it your business to be an authority on the topic (fear not: once you finish this chapter, you will be).

3. **Don't feel as though you need to be apologetic when discussing maternity leave.** It is your legal right to take this leave, and employers should not be shaming women or making them feel like they are letting down the team because they are expanding their family.

4. **Don't expect to come back to the exact same job.** Your employer must only provide you with a comparable position within the organization. You have the right to earn the same amount and to not be demoted from a supervisory/management position when you return from leave. Acknowledge that the organization may have to shift to fill your shoes while you are gone, and explain that while it would be your preference to get your specific job back, you are prepared to return to the comparable position you're entitled to.

5. **Be clear with them about how much leave you intend to take.** While it is true that employment standards legislation sets minimum requirements that you have to follow when providing notice that you are returning to work from maternity leave, practically speaking the more notice you can give about your plans, the easier the transition will be for your company.

6. **Be an active participant in the process of transitioning your work to someone else during your leave.** If possible, ask to participate in interviews to hire your replacement while you are on leave. Not only will this show that you are committed and invested in having your work carried out by someone competent while you are gone, but you can also advance your own career by helping to prepare a comprehensive job description that outlines all of your current duties and responsibilities. Your manager/boss may not really appreciate all that you do, and by drafting a job description for the person who will be filling in for you, you can help to highlight all of your valuable contributions to the company. If no replacement is being hired, then work very closely with the other employees on your team who will be taking over files or aspects of your work for you. Again, working closely with these people will create goodwill and show that you are invested in making your leave as smooth as possible for them.

Although it is illegal for an employer to fire an employee who's on maternity leave or to provide them with a lesser position upon their return, we have all heard horror stories of employers who did whatever they wanted and essentially dared the employee to sue them. Building a stronger relationship with your employer in the time leading up to your maternity leave—in regard to how and when you announce your pregnancy and what you do to assist in planning for your leave—will hopefully make them see you as a valued employee and think carefully before they act.

Okay, awesome. Thanks for the tips! you're thinking. *So what exactly am I entitled to under the law as it pertains to maternity/parental leave?*

OMG, we're so glad you asked! According to Sarah, these are your rights:

- Employment standards legislation across Canada has guaranteed the rights of employees to take maternity leave and parental leave (so yes, this applies to both moms and dads), and the rights outlined in employment standards legislation (e.g., the Employment Standards Act in Ontario, the Employment Standards Code in Alberta) are the minimum standards that employers have to follow. So regardless of what is in your contract, your employer cannot attempt to ignore the rights outlined in employment standards legislation; it would be illegal for them to do that. Company policies around how much notice an employee needs to give an employer before taking leave or whether or not the company will top up your pay while you are gone are certainly open for flexibility and negotiation, but your right to take up to 18 months' leave cannot be taken away from you.

- Employment standards legislation requires your employer to give you a comparable position upon your return to work. What is "comparable" is going to depend on the circumstances, but it generally means a position that is similar in terms of duties and responsibilities, and your pay and other compensation should not be changed.

- In addition to employment standards legislation, the common law in Canada—which is the law developed by judges through legal precedents and other cases that come before the courts—further protects you from being terminated while you are on maternity leave or parental leave.

- If your employer terminates you while you are on maternity leave or parental leave, it constitutes a wrongful dismissal at law. In addition to being entitled to receive damages equivalent to the pay you should have received at the end of your leave had your position been properly terminated then, you could also be entitled to aggravated damages.

- If your company goes through downsizing or restructuring while you are on maternity leave and your position is eliminated, your employer is *not* permitted to give you a severance package while you are on maternity leave—they are required to wait until you have finished your leave and then formally end your employment and provide you with a severance package. The main reason for this is a bit complicated, but it is important to understand: There is a presumption in law that an employee who loses their job due to no fault of their own (i.e., a without-cause termination, or as people sometimes call it, "a permanent layoff") is entitled to reasonable notice that the termination is coming so that they can look for a comparable position elsewhere (employers can attempt to contract out of this presumption, but most fail to properly do so). How much notice is "reasonable" depends on the facts of each situation (i.e., it varies based on your age, length of service, nature of your employment, and how easy or difficult it will be for you to find a comparable job based on the availability of similar positions). Most employers choose to provide pay in lieu of notice to their employees, but whether or not notice of termination or pay in lieu of notice is provided, the underlying rationale is the same: *An employee is entitled to have paid time to look for a comparable job.* While an employee is on maternity leave or parental leave, they are not going to be looking for another job, because they are on leave and are occupied with the all-consuming task of keeping a little person alive. Your reasonable notice period does not come into effect until you are able to look for work elsewhere, and as such, even if the company is going through downsizing, you have the right to not have your maternity leave or parental leave interfered with, and you can only be packaged out once your leave has ended. This requirement provides you with further job security while you are on leave.

- Human rights legislation provides further protection with respect to an employee's right to take maternity leave or parental leave.

Human rights legislation across Canada has stated that protected characteristics under the legislation include gender and family status, and case law has interpreted gender and family status to include pregnancy, maternity leave, and parental leave. If an employer tries to penalize you or fire you because you are pregnant or taking maternity leave or parental leave, it is discriminatory and illegal under human rights legislation, and you can file a complaint against your employer. Damages awards for human rights complaints include not only the income that you lost as a result of being discriminated against, but also general damages (read: tax-free money) for the injury to your dignity and sense of self-worth that you experienced because you were discriminated against.

- A potential employer should not ask you whether or not you have kids, mostly because if you don't get the job, you could point to the fact that they asked you about your family as evidence of discrimination on the basis of the protected ground of family status. Of course, that does not mean that if you are not the successful candidate for a job, it was automatically as a result of your status as a parent, but an employer should want to avoid any potential liability whatsoever by keeping the interview focused strictly on the job, rather than on your personal life. Now, that said, if you are the successful candidate and you would need certain accommodations in order to properly do your job, then you should certainly disclose that to your employer. Employers do have an obligation to accommodate personal circumstances within reason because failure to do so could give rise to a complaint of discrimination. For example, if the employer's hours of work are typically 8:30 a.m. to 4:30 p.m., but you need to leave work by 4:00 p.m. each day in order to pick up your children from school, the employer should accommodate a schedule of 8:00 a.m. to 4:00 p.m. unless doing so would cause undue hardship.

Resuming an Old Job as a New Woman

Returning to your old gig is likely to feel exhilarating, exhausting, reward-ing, frustrating, freeing, and confining—all at the same time. Just the act of heading out the door (and away from your baby, with whom you have spent nothing but one-on-one time for the past few months) can feel incredibly foreign. No matter how difficult this adjustment feels at the beginning, hang in there, Mama. Once everyone is on a schedule that makes sense for the whole family, the motions will become more fluid and you *will* find your groove again. Promise.

Re-Entering the Corporate World

Good News	Bad News
Your independence is back.	Your shit-head boss is back, too.
You are now acutely aware of how valuable your time is.	Unnecessary meetings and conference calls feel infinitely worse as a result.
Hot coffee! Whenever you want it!	Dehydration. So much dehydration.
You feel like you've gotten back some semblance of a social life again.	You hate all these fucking people.

Advocating for Yourself at Work

There is a good chance that once you get past the initial back-to-work hump, you'll find that you've settled into a routine that doesn't feel quite suitable. That's okay—and it is absolutely possible to request a new work schedule, style, or duties, without negatively impacting your standing . . . but it does take some preparation before you sit down to discuss it with your superiors. We recommend following this advice from Lauren Smith Brody, who specializes in helping women integrate back into the workforce.

Don't assume you have to take a pay cut. If you are hoping to achieve more flexibility in your schedule, you're going to want to know exactly what's in your job description and figure out how you can deliver that in the context of what you're requesting. Will you be working the same total number of hours? Will you be responsible for the same deliverables? Will less commuting time give you more work hours? Lean into *that*. Also, ask around to determine what precedent has been set by other employees, formally or not, and fold this intel into your proposed plan. Working fewer hours in-office doesn't necessarily mean you need to pro-rate your salary—but your company will likely take the opportunity to do so unless you resist.

Keep your full-time status. To be honest, this is less about your paycheque and more about your employer's RRSP contributions. When you maintain full-time status—which at many workplaces means only 35, or even 28, hours per week—you preserve your full benefits, the loss of which is a major contributor to the Motherhood Penalty. Do the math on the value of things like your paid time off, RRSP, and dental care, and you may find that it's well worth banging out a few extra hours to count as full-time. If your company needs to make layoffs down the line, your full-time status may save you.

Beware the flex Friday. If you want to work from home one day a week or use flexible hours, don't automatically grant yourself a three-day weekend until you've assessed your workplace's "calendar culture." Skipping a more random or "slower" day might be a better bet. Plus, as people tie off their weeks, there's often a flurry of finish-line crossing that can keep you from getting full credit for the previous four days of work.

Make it a trial period if you must. If you're sensing managerial resistance that's threatening your efforts to get what you want, suggest that you try this plan temporarily, with a check-in date after a few months so both sides can reassess. If you maintain your performance during this critical trial period, it's far less likely that you'll lose any of the ground you've gained.

Don't be afraid to call people out on their biases, which are often well-intended. Practise this sentence: "I appreciate your sensitivity to my new circumstance, but please don't count me out—I'd always like the option to decide whether to take on more work."

Changing Fields in a Corporate Landscape

If you did some real soul searching over the course of your pregnancy and parental leave and you decided that you're simply no longer fulfilled by your old job and you're ready to try something new professionally, we tip our hats to you. It is not uncommon for change to beget change, and since you've just undergone the largest shift known to humankind—parenthood—it's both understandable and commendable that you're willing to take yet another leap into the unknown. Go, you!

If you're changing fields, you'll first want to take inventory of your passions and your life goals to help you establish your new direction. Then you'll want to start researching new professions (check out Glassdoor for insight into different company cultures), talking to headhunters, exploring new certification options, and getting yourself set up properly on networking platforms like LinkedIn and Indeed. All of the above can be done via the power of the internet while your baby is napping (hallelujah!).

The most tedious aspect of changing fields is going to be the dreaded resumé creation. Depending on the field you're hoping to break into, you'll want to follow some pretty different guidelines when putting together a solid CV, but no matter what, there are a few key essentials you'll want to include.

Keep in mind that job applications today are often done through online form submissions, but it's good to have your resumé on hand to reference as you complete the process.

Building Your Resumé (from the Ground Up)

Don't forget your contact information. Duh! You need to make it as easy as possible for future employers to get a hold of you. This info needs to be front and centre—right at the top of your resumé. You'll want to include your phone number and email address. You may also consider including your home address (although it's not mandatory) and your website address (if applicable) to help employers access additional information about you quickly.

Go for clean and minimal. One of the most important elements of a resumé is easy readability, since employers and hiring managers don't have much time to read each individual resumé they receive. Your goal should be to help the reader take in a lot of important information about you in just a quick glance. For that reason, make sure it's laid out clearly, with a simple font that is large enough to read (aim for 10 to 12 point). Also, make sure to use bullet points in lieu of paragraphs—they're much easier for readers to digest.

Detail relevant experience only. It may be tempting to go into detail about every job you've ever had, but you're better off listing only the most relevant ones. Under each, briefly describe daily duties, but make sure to also list your most important accomplishments, standout results, and contributions. Think about how the things you achieved in previous jobs relate to what you'll try to achieve in the position you're applying for—that's what you'll want to highlight.

List skills. Do you know how to use a certain complicated software related to your industry? Or, are you an experienced photographer with a strong visual background? Think about the things that you can do that make you particularly suited for the position you're applying for, then write them down. This is a good way to set yourself apart from your competition.

Include post-secondary education experience. Any academic credential beyond a high school diploma should be included on your resumé. Nothing crazy—just list the institution(s) you attended, degree(s) you received, and your major(s). Educational experience should be located at the bottom of your resumé, after your professional experience.

No matter what kind of job you're applying for, simply focus on crafting a clean, brief resumé that highlights how well qualified you are for the position. There's a good chance that the process will happen online, which is why it's important to know your audience well and prepare the right resumé for the right job. Pair it with a well-written cover letter and you're good to go.

"But what about the mat leave gap?" you ask. Make like a PR maven and spin that shit into a positive. These gaps, after all, are usually filled with amazing experiences that will contribute to your own success and may help your employer gain a new perspective.

Yes, you may need a refresher on the newest social media app or a training sesh on the updated office software, but the important attributes will already be there: problem solving, multitasking, flexibility, work ethic, efficiency, productivity, etc. Use that gap on your resumé to *highlight* your mom skills—after all, it's the hardest job in the world, and you did it with no training.

The Rebel Mama Resumé

Objective:
To keep everyone happy and fucking quiet.

Skills:
Diplomacy. All of the diplomacy.
Fluency in multiple languages, including "safari lion" and
     "ninja alien."
Level 10 multitasking and on-the-fly problem solving.
Hardcore efficiency.
High tolerance for excruciating screams; prolonged, torture-inducing whine
     sessions; and small-toy injuries.
Infinite patience.
Expertise in strategic organization and delegation.
Laser-beam eyes that reach fifty metres and can be felt by the target even
     when they're turned away.

Special Talents:
Able to locate good wine (and/or sativa strain) in a hurry.

Able to answer 150 unrelated questions about life in under a minute.
Able to organize grocery list by store layout.
Able to prepare Master Chef meals when half the ingredients are missing.
Able to expertly time food delivery to arrive at the front door after school.

Qualifications:
Can produce profound words of wisdom at the drop of a hat.
Can mimic a multitude of TV character voices.
Can kiss all the boo-boos away.
Can roll a tight joint under pressure.
Has a dry sense of humour and hard eye roll.

Work Experience:
Hiding in a corner of the house after the kids have gone to bed and creating a badass business plan that will change the world while doing YouTube pilates and folding laundry and going upstairs to check on the food once in a while and considering the state of the world and how it will affect our children—in addition to four years of expert-level Lego City project management.

Volunteer Experience:
Dispensing personal time like goddamn PEZ.

Honours and Awards:
Cheerios necklaces.
Beads and marbles.
Stolen garden flowers.
Random sticks.
Hugs and kisses.
Butt slaps.

If interested, call me.
(But only between the hours of 9:00 and 11:00 p.m.)

Still stressing about it? We get it. That's why we called up our friend (and tech recruiter) Abby Goldstein for her input on the mat leave gap from the perspective of the employer. Here's what she had to say:

You want to work for a company culture that won't look at mat leave as a negative. Hiring managers are generally sympathetic, and interviews are about finding a good fit, not just about getting a job. The more honest and upfront you are about your mat leave gap, the better chance you have of finding an environment that you are happy in and a position that will allow you to succeed. If you have time, you might want to look at some of the trends in the industry and brush up on a new skill or get certified in an area that might be important. Finally, don't be afraid to leverage and expand on your network by reaching out and having continuous conversations, even "virtual coffees." You'd be surprised at how many people are willing to help.

Sometimes hiring managers worry that returning women aren't capable, wrongly assuming their skills have expired, their flexibility is lacking, and their commitment to the job is dwindling. Well, we don't have to tell you, babe: That's simply untrue. If anything, mamas have a shit-ton to contribute and the companies with the foresight to see that will reap the biggest rewards.

Insider Tips for Landing Your Dream Gig

For Agency Jobs

Don't be shy about adding visual elements to a resumé if you're submitting one, and make sure you have a solid cover letter detailing your applicable skills and interest in the field. Focus on your career highlights up to this point without getting too technical. The agency world focuses on effective project management, creative strategy, and account management, a.k.a. organizational, creative, and people skills. Showcase how you excel in these areas. And remember: "Culture eats creative for breakfast." Show that you are a team player and do so in a visually striking way.

For Media Jobs

Build an online portfolio for yourself—a basic website or blog format will do the trick. This way you can choose how to display your work and you can include as many examples of photos, videos, and copywriting as you want.

Also, practise what you preach! To work in media, one must fully understand the importance of communication, empathy, and storytelling. Convey this and you will pique interest.

For Sales Jobs

"Sell me this pen!" It's often hardest to sell ourselves, but taking a step back and looking at our accomplishments in an objective way can offer insight as to what to share with prospective employers. Focus on wins and the ROI you've brought in the past. Just make sure your resumé not only focuses on numbers, but also highlights strength in communication and relationship building.

For Tech Jobs

Make yourself aware of company culture specifics and showcase that you are up to date with the latest tech programs and industry advances, and how they can be incorporated with/into softer skills.

For Management Jobs

Highlight planning, organization, communication, and problem solving. Offer "anecdotes" on some of your managerial "wins" and "learnings."

The popular online job site Indeed.com recommends preparing in the following ways:

1. **Do your prep work.** Use the job description as a guide. Align with the details so you stand out as a solid candidate, and imagine what kinds of questions may come up in the interview; prepare concise answers.

2. **Know your "why."** Think about *why* you want this position and *what* qualifies you specifically. Practise answering those two questions until it feels natural.

3. **Understand the company.** Know their offering. Take time to understand the position you're applying for. Research company culture. Do a deep dive into their social media and blogs to understand tone, personality, and core values. If you're going to be part of the team, you want to be a good match.

4. **Prepare an elevator pitch.** Two sentences should be enough to describe who you are, what you do, and what you want. This is a big part of making a solid first impression. Practise a few times in the mirror before bringing it into the boardroom.

5. **Don't be late.** If the interview is in another part of town that you may not know well, take the time to organize your travel plans so you don't show up sweaty and defeated. Leave mega early, and if you get there ahead of time, use the extra minutes to prep.

6. **Practise good hygiene.** The devil is in the details, ladies. Refrain from overly strong perfumes, and keep your hair and nails neat and your makeup clean.

7. **Dress appropriately.** Creep potential co-workers on LinkedIn or check the "About" tab on a company website for a glimpse into their office style. If everyone's rockin' a crewneck, there's no need to interview in a power suit.

8. **Play the part.** Perfect your speaking voice and body language. Pay special attention to your smile, handshake (if people are still even doing that), and stride. Aim to exude a calm confidence. It's super awkward at first, but once you get comfortable using an assertive tone (we recommend speaking slower than you're used to) and friendly body language, you'll feel much more confident. Step it up a notch and record your trial runs in selfie mode to see where you can improve.

9. **Sell yourself.** If you have specific metrics to back up your accomplishments, like sales growth or increased customer engagement, throw those babies into the mix. They are concrete examples of how you can contribute to the company's success.

10. **Ask questions.** Don't interrupt the interviewer, of course, but if questions come up during the conversation, jot them down on a notepad and ask away at the end. This is about a good fit for both parties, so the more you know up front, the better.

Follow-Up Email Tips

(So you don't waste too much time obsessing before hitting Send.)

- Mention the job title, and thank your contact for the interview.

- Use a conversation point that seemed especially important to the interviewer, and connect that point to your qualifications/experience.

- Offer to answer any additional questions, and close by saying you're looking forward to hearing back.

According to the internet, this follow-up email should be sent no later than 24 hours after the interview to all participants. And don't ramble. Make sure you take your time editing this one.

Hot Girl Break!*

Recounting everything you've ever done, building a resumé from the ground up, and prepping for interviews ain't no easy feat. You deserve some sexy vibes for your efforts.

*('cause we believe love is love, OBV)

THE HU$TLER

Pros	Cons
Leaving an unfulfilling job after taking parental leave	Losing status and seniority along with it
Finding an enjoyable job with more flexibility OR creating a job by starting a new business	$2,000 monthly paycheque and no benefits OR new business is revenue negative for at least the first year
Pure fulfillment	Pure exhaustion
A partner who earns enough to sustain a financial hit while still living comfortably	Feelings of inadequacy due to contributing less financially
A schedule that can be flexible and bend around family needs	A family that doesn't value your time
Only requiring part-time paid childcare, costing under $1,000 per month	Some months barely breaking even
Working remotely	Working constantly
Paying very little in taxes and likely qualifying for sizable tax benefits	Earning very little but putting in full-time (plus) hours between working and caretaking
Paying down debts and saving strategically once childcare expenses are alleviated (when youngest child goes to school)	Losing years of valuable time benefiting from compound interest on savings getting to that point

Hot Tips for Hu$tlers

- Make sure your partner takes parental leave or you will 100 percent become the default parent for everything, for the rest of your life.

- Before you take this plunge into the unknown, make sure you've got a financial plan outlined with your partner (for a refresher on ways to amalgamate funds, refer to page 13).

- Prepare for relationship drama to materialize. We tend to take stress out on our partners, and walking away from steady income in exchange for random payouts is stressful AF. Be clear about your goals and keep communication as open as possible.

- If you do not have a partner, seriously consider the financial risk you'd be taking by becoming a freelance professional and forfeiting regular income (and likely benefits) for the foreseeable future.

- As soon as you can afford to outsource home maintenance (i.e., hire a cleaner), do it. You'll be shocked at the time it will free up.

- Find yourself a mentor who has taken a similar path to success and made it. They will help you navigate the shitstorm of juggling hustling with parenting.

- Know that starting a business is majorly time-consuming and often resource-sucking. Prepare yourself for this reality. Working part-time while starting a business isn't the worst idea—at least until you're making enough money to cover the absolute basics while you get your endeavour off the ground.

- Get comfortable with the fact that the next few years are not going to be "money making" years—they are "staying alive" years. You may have to take on new debt. You may dip deep into your savings or have to refinance your house to keep your head above water, but if you're making consistent money and it looks like your idea is really growing into something promising, then consider the time spent keeping yourself in the game throughout your kids' early childhood an investment in your future.

- Be honest with yourself and your stakeholders—this applies to both your partner in life and your partner in business. Financial transparency with your partners is a must; once that's out of the way, then you can come up with a plan.

Exploring Entrepreneurship

Entrepreneurship sounds fun, and social media has a tendency to make it look alluring AF, but if it's something you are considering, we encourage you to be practical and logical when deciding if this pipe dream has any legs and whether you can realistically afford to chase it. Being an entrepreneur often means seeing no profit for four to five years, and you need to be real about whether that's something you and your family can feasibly sustain.

The Good News	The Bad News
You'll be able to work from home in your best pyjamas and never be micromanaged again.	Not only is the future of your business in your hands, so is your next paycheque.
You get to finally do something you are passionate about and execute it exactly the way you like.	If your start-up business fails, you'll lose your savings, time, and effort. (In Canada, 57 percent of start-ups fail within five years.)
All the profits are yours! Eureka! You don't have to split your earnings with anyone.	It takes forever for any actual profit to roll in, and since all the debt is solely resting on your shoulders, it gets paid into first. Whomp whomp.
You get to make boss-babe decisions all day about your brand/product, your strategy, and your ethos. Plus, you get to expense your own martini lunches.	Since the workload is solely yours and since it's a serious hustle (especially at the beginning), it can become overwhelming if not organized properly, and those martini lunches will drop to the bottom of the priority list quick.
You can dictate your own schedule and work whatever hours you like!	Forget the 40-hour workweek. This bitch will dominate your life.
You can finally be the leader you've always imagined yourself to be! (Prada power suit and all.)	You are accountable for 100 percent of your business's success, and if that means learning new skills on the fly, then, honey, that's just part of your job now.
You won't have to listen to anyone's unsolicited opinion about anything you're doing.	You will de facto need a shitload of business advice, so get used to asking for it.

The only easy thing about entrepreneurship is that you don't need to compile a resumé and get hired by someone in order to start. You simply need to expel an idea from your brain and develop a plan to make it happen. NBD, right?

(Don't worry, babe. You can do it! We believe in you.)

Once you've done that, you'll need to decide how you're registering this business of yours. In Canada, you can either do so as a sole proprietorship/ partnership or you can register as a corporation. Both options allow you to operate business, but they cost different amounts to set up and are governed by different tax laws.

Let's start with the basic business package:

Sole Proprietorship/Partnership

These are two forms of the same kind of business: "Sole proprietorship" means you're founding it alone, while "partnership" means you're founding it with others. Either way, this kind of business is attached to your personal banking and SIN. It is an extension of your personal finances. If you're just starting out, this is a totally fine option to begin with. It gives you the flexibility to make business deposits to your personal account directly if needed but also supplies with you the credentials to open business accounts and start setting yourself up properly. When you file your taxes, yours and the business's taxes are considered one and the same, and filing is simple.

And now for the slightly more robust business package:

Corporation

Registering your company as a corporation, or "incorporating," is a smart thing to do if your first order of business is flushing your company with cash through a round of funding from venture capitalists or a big loan from the bank. (This is where that low debt-to-income ratio and excellent credit score will come in handy, BTW. More on that later.) Incorporating basically allows you to form an entirely new entity for the company you're creating. It may be founded and operated by you, but is not an extension of you—you are legally detached from it, enough so that you're protected from things like having to file personal bankruptcy if the business fails (unlike sole proprietorships, corporations can go bankrupt with little to no threat to their owners' personal credit). A corporation can also be set up in a way to accommodate outside investors—typically, these parties will buy a piece of your company (or a "common share") as an investment. Keep in mind that anyone looking to invest in your company will be doing so because of their own financial interests, coupled with their belief in you and desire to see you succeed. If you're looking to outsource cash flow to get a business off the ground, you'll want to come prepared with cost and revenue projections and a very detailed plan as to how you intend to make this thing work. (This task may take a few months to create, so factor that in.)

If you're gonna do it, do it right.

Here's where we are going to tell you that no matter what kind of business you're registered as, the added expense of a lawyer and accountant are absolutely worth the investment. Lawyers understand the law as it pertains to your business; accountants understand the law as it pertains to your money—the good ones do, anyway—and they'll help you navigate all the loopholes for keeping your hard-earned cash in your pocket. Unless you yourself have a strong background in either of these areas, we suggest flipping this one over to the professionals. Strapped for cash at the moment? Ask around—maybe there's someone in your social circle who's willing to help (and give you a better rate) to get you started on the right foot. If not, research companies specializing in small business services—they'll have much better rates than the big guys and will be able to provide more personalized assistance.

The key here is to set everything up properly in order to avoid major—and we mean *major*—drama in the future. No one wants to suddenly owe the government thousands of dollars or get involved in a lawsuit down the line because of a few contractual oversights. It's boring as shit, but paperwork needs to be organized and filed accurately or you are putting your business at risk.

Accounting services include managing the books; making sure procedures comply with government regulations; tracking and filing expenses; advising on financial plans and statements; creating year-end financial reports; submitting taxes; and managing payroll, invoicing, and collections. Accountants also determine areas of growth, help prevent audits, and provide financial forecasts.

Legal services include determining the best business structure; registering the business name; applying for necessary trademarks; drafting NDAs (non-disclosure agreements), SAs (shareholder agreements), ECs (employee contracts), and licensing agreements; and complying with laws and regulations. Lawyers also provide trustworthy legal advice, protect your intellectual property, advise on potential liabilities, and offer best business practices.

As you can see, these folks are good to have in your corner as they can offer you the kind of valuable advice that may very well save your ass one day. And we're all about a good ass saving.

Getting Paid (in a Relatively Timely Manner)

Let's be real: When you're a parent living in chaos and trying to simultaneously get a business off the ground, shit gets overlooked. You create your invoice, send it off to your client, and pretty much forget about it until your bank account starts looking miserable, and you're suddenly searching through emails wondering when payments were due. We've been there, girl, and it wasn't good for the health of our business or our emotional well-being. We want to equip you with some practical tips to help you get paid so you can continue with your badassery:

- Before you work with anyone, do some background digging. Do they have a good reputation? Do they pay on time? Ask around.

- Draft up a basic contract to hold both parties accountable for deliverables (i.e., your service for their money).

- Sign up for an invoicing service online like QuickBooks or PayPal— they make it easy to manage and follow up if need be.

- If you don't have the budget or the desire to do your invoicing online, set up your invoices in Google or Excel sheets so they are easy to replicate and save.

- Keep all your invoices filed and organized in a folder on your desktop. This also serves as a reminder every time you flip your laptop open that someone may owe you money.

- Include the due date on the invoice (typically 30 to 60 days). Some larger corporations require 90 days, so just be aware and budget accordingly.

- Include the due date in the email when you send the invoice.

- Since it may be slightly awkward invoicing personally, we recommend you send these from an info@ or accounting@ email address that keeps things neutral (i.e., play your own assistant).

- Include any deposits due upon signing to ensure you don't do all the work up front before getting paid (25 to 50 percent is reasonable).

- Include late fees at the bottom of your invoice once it has gone past the due date. (Note: This is difficult to execute in practice as most people simply DGAF.)

- Follow up with a friendly email once the invoice is due. Set a reminder in your phone so you don't miss it.

- If you're having a hard time getting the cash, have your accountant follow up in a less friendly but still professional way (or just pretend to be your own assistant again and do it yourself).

- Still not getting paid? Show up at their office with Rihanna's "Bitch Better Have My Money" blasting through your earbuds and ride that vibe all the way to the bank.

- Don't actually do that. If you get stiffed on the invoice completely, seek legal action. This where your lawyer comes in handy (again).

THE $CHOLAR

Pros	Cons
Chasing goals and dreams	Doing it on three hours of sleep per day
Enriched mind	A brain that feels like mush 95 percent of the time
Increased future earning potential	Demolished current earning potential and social life
Qualifying for grants to pay for school/apprenticeships	Grants only give money, not extra energy or hours in the day. Sorry.
Being a positive role model to kids	Sacrificing a lot of time spent with said kids over the course of your education
Proving to yourself that you can do anything you put your mind to	Staring down a seemingly endless stream of obstacles
A break from the mom-grind	Even more shit to do in a day

Hot Tips for $cholars

- Look into programs that have both on-campus and online elements—the more control you have over your schedule, the better.

- See if you qualify for daycare subsidies because of your student status.

- Ensure you have some form of support system in place to help take care of the kids. (This can look like any combo of paid help, grandparent help, spouse help, and friends help. This undertaking seriously does take a village.)

- Time management will be key, so make sure you have all important dates marked on a calendar that all family members can access.

- Establish a good rapport with your professors and ensure they understand your situation.

- If you need an extension on an assignment, ask for it as early as possible and be transparent about your reasoning to your profs and TAs.

- You'll probably have to sacrifice some of your social life and stuff like watching TV, but once you get over the initial hump, you won't miss either.

- Remember that you can set your own pace. A degree earned over seven years is still a degree earned.

- School will eat up a lot of the time you would normally dedicate to maintaining your home or cooking meals. Lower your expectations significantly in those departments for the duration of your education. Something's gotta give.

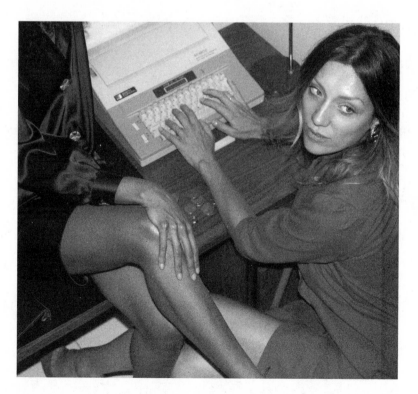

Academic Loans and Grants

So, you want to make like Billy Madison and go back to school, huh? Well, good on you, sister! Education and apprenticeship training provide access to well-paid jobs and exciting career prospects, and luckily, there are several loans and grants out there that were designed to help you access that shit without going broke.

In Canada, loans and grants for college are all dealt with on a provincial basis, so to get started, you should get an application form from your local office and send it in for assessment for a student loan. You can find the relevant offices for each province at www.canlearn.ca. In most cases you will be able to apply online. Once you have made a loan application, you will be able to be assessed for grant eligibility, too. Keep in mind that loans must be paid back, so make sure you understand all the terms and conditions completely. Grants, on the other hand, are basically free money that you never have to pay back, so if you can get one, take it!

Here are a few of the most popular grants in Canada:

The Canada Student Grant for Full-Time Students

This grant is available to students from low- and middle-income families who are enrolled in a full-time undergraduate program at a designated post-secondary institution. You could receive up to $3,000 per eight-month school year (up to $375 per month of study). You can receive this grant for each year of your undergraduate studies if you still qualify.

You are eligible if you can check all four of the following boxes:

☐ You apply and qualify for student financial assistance.

☐ You do not live in Northwest Territories, Nunavut, or Quebec (they have their own student aid programs).

☐ You are enrolled as a full-time student in an undergraduate degree, diploma, or certificate program that is at least two years (60 weeks) in duration at a designated post-secondary institution.

☐ Your total family income is less than the income threshold outlined by the government of Canada.

The Canada Student Grant for Part-Time Students

This grant is available to low- and middle-income part-time students enrolled in a program at a designated post-secondary institution, including studies beyond the undergraduate level. You could receive up to $1,800 each school year (August 1 to July 31). You can get this grant for each year of your studies (including undergraduate and graduate levels) if you still qualify.

You are eligible if you can check all four of the following boxes:

☐ You apply and qualify for part-time student financial assistance.

☐ You are enrolled as a part-time student in a degree, diploma, or certificate program (at least 12 weeks long within a period of 15 weeks) at a designated post-secondary institution, including studies beyond the undergraduate level.

☐ You have successfully completed all courses for which you previously received a grant.

☐ Your total family income is less than the income threshold outlined by the government of Canada.

The Canada Student Grant for Full-Time Students with Dependants

This grant is available to low-income students with dependants while they're enrolled in a full-time program at a designated post-secondary institution. You could receive up to $200 each month for every dependent child you have per year of full-time studies. This amount is in addition to the Canada Student Grant for Full-Time Students.

For example, if you qualify for a government grant and you have an assessed need of $3,000, you will receive a Canada Student Grant for Full-Time Students with Dependants of $1,600 per child ($200 per month of study) in addition to the Canada Student Grant for Full-Time Students of $3,000 ($375 per month of study), assuming you study for eight months.

You are eligible if you can check all four of the following boxes:

☐ You apply and qualify for student financial assistance.

☐ You are enrolled as a full-time student in a degree, diploma, or certificate program that is at least two years (60 weeks) in duration at a designated post-secondary institution, including studies beyond the undergraduate level.

☐ You have a dependant who will be under 12 years of age at the beginning of the study period (or a dependant 12 years of age or older with a permanent disability).

☐ Your total family income is less than the income threshold outlined by the government of Canada.

The Canada Student Grant for Part-Time Students with Dependants

This grant is available to low- and middle-income part-time students with dependants while they are enrolled in a program at a designated post-secondary institution, including studies beyond the undergraduate level. You could receive up to $1,800 each school year (August 1 to July 31). You can get this grant for each year of your studies (including undergraduate and graduate levels) as long as you still qualify.

You are eligible if you can check all four of the following boxes:

☐ You apply and qualify for part-time student financial assistance.

☐ You are enrolled as a part-time student in a degree, diploma, or certificate program (at least 12 weeks long within a period of 15 weeks) at a designated post-secondary institution, including studies beyond the undergraduate level.

☐ You have a dependant who will be under 12 years of age at the start of the study period (or a dependant 12 years of age or older with a permanent disability).

☐ Your total family income is less than the income threshold outlined by the government of Canada.

In addition to all these generous programs available in Canada, there are also a plethora of merit-based scholarships for undergraduate, postgraduate, and post-doctoral studies, so go on, girl. Go get your learning on (and do it on someone else's dime if you can!).

Apprenticeships and Training

If you're interested in becoming a skilled tradesperson or craftsperson, you might be looking for an apprenticeship. An apprenticeship is an agreement between the apprentice, the employer, and the apprenticeship authority in the area where the work and training take place. Apprenticeships are an excellent way to develop the skills you need to obtain work in the future and are more specific to a trade than a general education. They usually involve long periods of on-the-job training (practical learning) and shorter periods of classroom study. An exam often takes place at the end of the training period (which is usually two to five years in length) depending on the trade. If you're just getting started, you'll find lots of apprenticeship info on the Government of Canada website. The most important thing to be aware of is whether or not you're choosing a Red Seal trade. Picking a Red Seal trade means that you can eventually apply for Red Seal certification, which allows you the freedom to work anywhere across Canada (you can find more information on that at www.red-seal.ca).

Luckily, there are a few grants that can be obtained in Canada for the funding of apprenticeships:

The Apprenticeship Incentive Grant (AIG)

This grant aims to encourage apprentices in the early stages of their training to continue through the course of the apprenticeship and reap the benefits.

So, after two full years of training (in a Red Seal program) have been completed, an award grant of $1,000 is made to the apprentice. This can be repeated for another year for a maximum payout of $2,000.

The Apprenticeship Completion Grant (ACG)

The rewards don't stop with the AIG in Canada. Once you've completed all your training, passed your exam, and become a qualified tradesperson, you are could be eligible for a further award of $2,000. Of course, you do have to have all your documents in place to prove that you have qualified fully, but it doesn't matter if you didn't collect the AIG first. And, if you're a keener who was able to fully complete your apprenticeship within a two-year period (brava!), you can claim both grants at the same time.

A RAPID-FIRE INTERVIEW WITH $CHOLAR DR. JACQUI WILKINS, ND

Professional Title: Naturopathic Doctor
MOM SINCE 2016

Can you give us some hot tips for managing your finances while in school?

The upside to finances while becoming a doctor and having a baby is that you literally don't have time for spending money or going out. I packed lunches, snacks, etc., for 12-hour shifts of seeing patients and studying. I opted for black coffee vs. expensive lattes (they add up!). I was also more likely to borrow than to buy baby stuff or I purchased second-hand. Good for the wallet and for the environment.

How did you manage childcare while in school?

Not very well! My little one's dad (who was also studying to be an ND at the time) was able to take different shifts so he could watch our babe while I was in clinic. I'd often have him hang out on campus with our son so I could continue nursing. We would rotate baby duty when studying for licensing exams: one of us staying up late and the other waking up early to study. We lived near school so if I needed to, I was able to drop in and ask some baby-friendly colleagues to watch him for an hour on campus if his dad couldn't.

Were you able to apply for grants?

No. As a US citizen on a student visa, I couldn't apply. Needless to say, I have a lot of student debt.

What did your support system look like?

Coffee? Ha! Friends, all the way. My supervisors were also super supportive. Of course, Rebel Mama Highchair Hangouts, too. Just knowing other parents were in it. I don't have family here, and that was challenging.

What roadblocks did you face and how did you get around them?

I had a bit of postpartum depression—I think from lack of sleep, lack of support, and the pressure of being a clinical intern/seeing patients. I sought out someone to talk with and reminded myself why I wanted to be a doctor, and a mama. Plant medicines and coffee helped with memory—it's amazing how childbirth affects our ability (or lack thereof) to retain information!

What would you have done differently if you did it again?

I would find more support . . . somehow. If I could have had family or friends who could watch my son more regularly, that would be key. I would also take care of my body better (easier said than done when barely functioning). Lastly, I would have been more compassionate with myself on the hard days.

So, chasing goals and dreams, babe . . . Was it worth it?

Absolutely! If we aren't working toward our dreams, what are we doing? Even if it means being tired for a few extra years. Our education will support us (and our communities) for a lifetime.

THE $AHM

Pros	Cons
Escaping from a professional life that no longer suits	Coming to find that your new life feels equally unsuitable
Developing a skill set to do the jobs of many	Getting paid $0.00 for all efforts
Making most of the decisions pertaining to the family and home	(Unpaid) emotional labour involved in making said decisions
Freeing family from the burden of paid childcare	Susceptible to losing sanity in the process
Freeing family from the burden of maintaining investments (like the home)	Feeling more like the family maid than the family matriarch
Spending unlimited time with kids	Days feel incredibly long. Years feel incredibly short.
Free time to relax and pursue hobbies	Hahahaha. Just kidding.
Saving household dollars by spending strategically	Desperately missing the days of not price matching at grocery stores
Exploring options for making money from home for the sake of having a personal stash	More likely to spend that money than save it when it arrives in the name of #selfcare

Hot Tips for $AHMs

- Closely assess your family's finances with your partner and establish that you can live comfortably off a single income for the foreseeable future before you resign from your job.

- Equitably share parental leave with your partner—you'll need them to have a reference point for the level of bullshit you deal with every day so they're less likely to step out of line with some "what do you even do all day?" fuckery.

- Merge finances if you haven't already and ensure you have full access to all family bank accounts.

- Maintain your own bank account, even if just money from random jobs goes into it from time to time. You'll want to maintain a small nest egg of savings that is just yours.

- Participate in family budgeting, and if you need to, take the lead.

- Get the entire family involved with household chores: You are a mother, not a maid. They may all need to be reminded of this repeatedly.

- If you can find room in the family budget for a housekeeper, you will find this is money well spent and may actually afford you some downtime in the day.

- If you want to embark on a creative endeavour, know that that will require quiet time alone to think. Prioritize this time and plan with your partner to ensure you get it.

If you grew up in the '70s, '80s, or '90s, you are very much familiar with the concept of the stay-at-home mom. If you didn't have one, you definitely knew a lot of them. Staying at home to raise kids was the working-middle-class ideal for most of our lives, and today we exist in a system in which mothers are often underpaid (thanks, wage gap!), in which childcare costs too much, and in which social pressure to be the primary parent simply because you're female is real. The urge to quit your job and become a full-time caretaker is common and understandable.

If you do choose to stay at home full-time, please just make sure it's for the only reason that matters: because you want to.

If you know deep down in your soul that this is what you want, sit down with your partner and have a very serious conversation about your family's financial situation and how you'll manage it going forward. Get involved.

We also encourage every $AHM to remain open to the idea of rejoining the workforce in some capacity, at some point. Financial dependence has been linked to some seriously sinister shit, like drug and alcohol abuse, anxiety, depression, and domestic violence. Financial independence, on the other hand, has been linked to great shit, like overall happiness and healthier relationships. Knowing that, perhaps we should explore some ways to make some extra scratch as a $AHM.

Note that you should have a clear plan outlined for any money you make through your part-time endeavour, whether it goes to family savings, home upgrades, extracurriculars, or anything in between. The goal of making your own money is to work toward your family's financial goals as well as to ensure your credit score remains in the "good" zone, notwithstanding your partner's financial dealings. Consider depositing earnings into an account that is strictly yours and then transferring to joint accounts after. Think about how you'd like to set yourself up for when the kids are in school and your earning potential increases.

Joining the Gig Economy

Wait . . . what exactly is this *gig economy* and is it really something for you? The gig economy is short-term or independent contract/freelance work as opposed to a permanent job. If you're not familiar with the term, it may just sound like a buzzword—but the steady growth of start-ups that support the gig economy and the advertising opportunities available on social media are indicators of how the working culture is growing and evolving. Depending on your needs and where you stand with your finances, this may just be a pretty sexy-looking option; it's a great way to earn part-time or supplementary income, it doesn't require large amounts of time, and payments usually come in quick.

The Good News	The Bad News
You'll have flexible hours.	They may be inconsistent AF.
You control the workload you can handle.	Because it's not full-time, you won't be eligible for any benefits.
You get to do something you're passionate about!	It's a hell of a lot less passion-inducing when you have to keep track of scheduling and irregular pay dates to make sure it's all accurate.
If you try something new, you may find a new passion!	Or you may rage-hate the first thing you try, but hey, tomorrow is another day, right?

Options will vary widely depending on what is ideal for you, but here are just a few gig ideas that could work. (Consider your personal interests, skills, and experience, OBV.)

- Copywriting
- Social media management
- Photography/editing
- Uber driving
- Dog walking
- Housekeeping
- Closet organization
- Private fitness/yoga classes
- Makeup artistry
- Handy work
- Private cooking classes
- Consulting
- Commercial/acting spots
- Tutoring
- Visual art and illustration

Not sure exactly where you fit in? Jot down some notes below and see where they lead you. We've found that this activity pairs well with a light sativa. Just sayin'.

What are you passionate about? Animals? Humans? Sustainability? Health? Food?

(Sleep, probably.)

_____

_____

What are your most impressive skills? Communication? Problem solving? Organization? Multitasking?

(Duh, you're a mom. Add all those.)

_____

_____

What are your interests? Technology? Arts/culture? Outdoor sports?

(No, Netflix and Chris Hemsworth aren't interests.)

_____

_____

What experience do you have? What did you do in the past? What are you good at now?

(Be willing to surprise yourself here, girl. You may have grown in unexpected ways.)

_____

_____

_____

Okay, so you've narrowed it down and have a few options.

Now, where are you going to find this work?

Shocking no one, there is a plethora of resources online, including LinkedIn, Indeed, and Facebook. You can also join apps like Jiffy on Demand and Uber with a few taps on your smartphone.

But don't be too quick to go completely online and discount the success rate of human contact. By merely telling people about the kind of work you're planning on doing/finding, you speak things into existence. And not only does this suddenly hold you accountable, but it may reveal unexpected opportunities in the least likely of places:

"Shut up, you're gonna start advertising your handywoman skills? That's amazing! Can you fix all the things I've been asking my husband to fix for the past four years? Yes? Fantastic! You're hired and I'm telling all my friends!"

BAM. Two hundred bucks. And who knows how much more moola to follow.

Remember, no matter what job you're doing, give it your *all*. Customer feedback is king, and your reputation will be key for referrals and recommendations. And don't forget to boast about it via Google Reviews if you're in business for yourself—people read that shit like it's gospel.

HOW TO BE IMPRESSIVE

be punctual
communicate clearly
prioritize efficiency
share ideas
exude passion
listen intently
work hard
be proactive
follow up
don't be a dick

A SMALL VICTORY: MOM OF ALL TRADES

By Lisa Corbo

Bella, don't let them tell you that you can't have it all. Listen to me. This your life. It's not a dress rehearsal. I say, go big or go home—set your own rules and believe in yourself because you can have it all.

In my 60 years on earth, I've been a textile designer, a fashion designer, and a two-time SAHM (each time on a different continent). I eventually re-entered the workforce full-time and have since built multiple successful businesses, collaborated with internationally renowned fashion designers, helped raise over $2 million for causes dear to my heart, launched an eponymous jewellery line, and somehow parented two amazing kids through the chaos. I've seen it all, learned it all, lost it all, had it all . . . And I'm just getting started.

As a young adult, it's entirely possible that I was the most driven woman in the world—all I cared about was my education and my career. The former I got at RMIT Melbourne, where I graduated as a textile designer, leading me to my passionate path in fashion. I won gown of the year in Australia, and the year I graduated, I took off, leaving Down Under behind.

All I wanted was to work and travel, and that's precisely what I did. I hopped from London to Paris to Rome until I met my Prince Charming, George, in Milan; he swept me off my feet and across the Atlantic.

Of course, I'm no fool, so before giving the definite "yes," I worked my international contacts and secured a brand development job at Holt Renfrew. I blinked and I was a bride in my hometown of Melbourne. A bride who then moved across the world and landed on two feet in Canada. As you can imagine, babies were not in my immediate plan. But then, just as my career got settled and everything was on the up and up, I discovered I was pregnant.

To be honest, I was never a baby lover. My personality lends itself more to children age five and above. I had no idea what to expect—but let me tell you, all that changed the moment I held my daughter for the first time. I was obsessed. Circumstances that year unfortunately took me back to Australia, so what I had planned on being a three-month maternity leave turned into a two-year hiatus. Finally, one night after having discussed the light bulb in the kitchen for over 60 minutes, my husband, George, gently indicated to me that it seemed the world of Barney had taken over my brain, and perhaps it was time to start focusing my energy on other things. I took his advice and I eased myself back into the world of fashion by opening and operating a studio boutique.

We settled into a great vibe. My daughter was older—four going on twenty. We travelled well together, and business was good. And then in the summer of '97, I came down with what I thought was the worst flu ever. I felt like hell for months and couldn't figure out what was wrong with me. As it turned out, it was no flu; it was pregnancy.

What do to, what to do? My husband and I sat down together and ran the numbers for all the different scenarios. We realized we could not afford to continue paying for childcare if I took time off. Financially, we were in a bind, and to be honest, I was in an emotional bind, too. As a mother, I felt a deep responsibility to (a) spend valuable time with my soon-to-be second child and (b) be there for my eldest as she adjusted to life with a sibling. And so, after much deliberation, I handed over the reins of the business we'd grown together to my husband. It was goodbye, nanny; Mama Lisa was back reporting for duty at the Corbo residence.

Truth be told: I loved it. My second was a much happier baby; I probably would have had additional children if he had been my first. I threw myself into the role of super mom. We did everything together: Art for Toddlers, Gym for Toddlers, Cooking for Toddlers, music class, swim class. You name it, we did it, and you better believe I was consistently overdressed for the occasion (by North American standards, anyway).

I did enjoy it for a while, though. It kept me busy, allowed me to spend more time with both kids, and helped me build a community in my neighbour-hood—a place where, thanks to my fresh-off-the-runway wardrobe and out-spoken tendencies, I was always considered to be a bit of a rebel. However, I learned that as much as my children needed me, they needed other people, too. I realized that we all needed more space—as a family—so I decided to try something new. I started to drop my son off at a part-time daycare a couple days a week. My daughter had started school (free childcare!) and in those small windows of time, I attempted to break into the wonderful world of interior design. I started with my ever-growing group of mom friends. I'd go to their houses and basically reorganize everything . . . but I'm pretty sure I never got paid a penny. Nevertheless, the gig taught me one very important thing: I needed to work if I wanted to be truly fulfilled.

When my kids were 11 and 8, I went all in. I hired a nanny/housekeeper (who is still working with me, a decade and a half later) to make sure the kids got from point A to point B in the morning and were well-fed and clean, while I began a new chapter in my life, once again as a working mom.

The truth of the matter is that I am at my best when I have an audience that I can style and that appreciates the art of dressing up. I love to play with the aesthetics that amplify a woman's being, so for the past 15 years, I've designed a life for myself wherein I can do just that. With grit, I admit, I have grown a multi-million-dollar small business with my husband that includes a successful eponymous jewellery line. I have styled some of the most iconic women in the world and raised over $2 million for Princess Margaret Hospital Cancer Research. (Oh, did I not mention I also survived melanoma through all of this? Ah, that's a story for another time.)

The point is this, ladies: You can have it all. You really can. The career, the glamour, the kids, the marriage, the life! I stayed at home with both my kids full-time for the first two years of each of their lives. I forged friendships that drifted apart and came back together decades later. I've started my career from scratch more times than I can count, in more countries than most people travel to in a lifetime. I've taken help when I needed it and lent a hand at every chance I've had, and my life is incredibly rich as a result. So I'll tell you again: You can have it all. It may not come all at once, it may not come the way you thought it would, the timing might suck, it might be scarier than you ever imagined it would be . . . Do it anyway.

Resist the boxes the world wants to put you in. Be bold. Love deeply. Take chances. Life is just one big fabulous adventure—trust your gut and enjoy the ride.

Imposter Syndrome (and How to Avoid Falling Victim to It)

Ah, imposter syndrome: the psychological roadblock we set for ourselves.

Imposter syndrome occurs among high achievers and reflects a belief that you're inadequate or incompetent despite clear evidence of the contrary. People experiencing imposter syndrome often attribute their accomplishments to luck rather than to ability and view themselves as frauds, especially among their colleagues. This phenomenon is real, people. It's diminishing, it's frustrating, it's inhibiting, and (feel free to not feign your surprise when we tell you this) it affects women—specifically women of colour—at a much higher rate than it does men.

It can also take various forms, depending on a person's background, personality, and circumstances.

Dr. Valerie Young, the current expert on the subject, categorizes people who suffer from imposter syndrome into five subgroups:

The Superwoman/man

- takes on an unconscionable amount of work;

- pushes to work harder than their peers (often putting their mental health in peril as a result); and

- is addicted to the validation that comes from working hard rather than the final output.

The Natural Genius

- sets incredibly high performance standards for themselves;

- believes they should get everything right on the first try; and

- is extremely hard on themselves if high standards are not met or exceeded.

The Soloist

- believes they should be able to do everything by themselves;

- refuses assistance to prove their worth; and

- is susceptible to burnout as a result of unnecessary workload.

The Expert

- measures their competence based on quantity of knowledge;

- endlessly seeks information to avoid seeming inexperienced or inept; and

- is fixated on learning to the point that it prevents them from *doing*.

The Perfectionist

- is never satisfied;

- always thinks they could have done better; and

- refuses to celebrate their own victories.

The common denominator here is self-doubt, something that can have an all-encompassing effect on our personal and professional lives. Doubt (and the worry that accompanies it) is a disaster for productivity—who has time to work when they're busy obsessing over all the ways they're not qualified for their job?—and it unsurprisingly acts as a massive career progression barrier to those who suffer from it. That's why it's so important to identify and address your own propensity toward imposter syndrome, pronto.

What can you do to address it? Lots of things! You can seek reassurance from someone who has witnessed your growth; teachers and mentors have a unique perspective and can help you mark your progress using tangible benchmarks. You can grab a pen and jot down a list of all your skills as well as all the areas in which you'd like to improve—this exercise will show you where there's legitimate room for improvement so you can stop walking around under a general "not good enough" cloud all day. You can try your hand at teaching. Mentoring/educating others is a great way to illuminate your skills and knowledge to yourself. At the end of the day, the more you see yourself in a positive light (even by way of your peers), the less likely you'll be to fall victim to your own mind fuckery.

But self-awareness aside, we'd be doing women a disservice if we ignored the fact that a doubt-filled internal dialogue is actually a logical response to a world that was not designed for women to succeed in professionally. Micro-aggressions enacted toward women (especially toward BIWOC) in both school and work environments create a false narrative that we are inferior. It's not an idea we're born with, but one we internalize over time. So while we must take responsibility for ourselves, our mindsets, and our actions, we cannot let ourselves fall into the trap of believing that the root of the problem is women's refusal to believe in themselves. It runs a hell of a lot deeper than that.

Making It Work, Equitably

Women today are living in a new world of female power and independence. We're busting through glass ceilings, rewriting old rules, creating new opportunities, and expressing ourselves physically, sexually, and intellectually in ways never seen before. But look just below the surface and you'll find that under these new developments lie the same conventions around mating and marriage that were popular in the 1950s.

So what's to blame here? Are all male partners just assholes? Are moms really just better at doing all the mental and emotional "stuff" that children require us as parents to do? No and no. The problem is that this "balance" we're all attempting—of having a domestic life and a public life—*is a relatively new phenomenon*, and as a result we are still grappling with antiquated biases that result in heavier workloads for women in general and moms specifically.

Today, approximately 75 percent of women in a heterosexual two-parent American household are likely to contribute to household finances and 22 percent of women are the breadwinners. But we're still spending almost twice the amount of time that men do (14 hours a week) on childcare and house chores, while fathers use time off for hobbies and relaxing.

What we're failing to do as a society is to draw a line connecting the above statistics with the fact that women are burning out at alarming rates. We're medicated. We're depressed. As a demographic, we're underrepresented in all the top earning/most powerful positions in the corporate, scientific, and political world. We're also the most vulnerable majority out there.

But before you start thinking that this is an environment wherein men, by comparison, should be thriving, you better think again. As a group, men are grappling with the unfortunate legacy of male "toughness"—they have the highest rates of suicide and the highest propensity toward gun violence. They are under immense pressure to provide materially for their family, and they're often denied opportunities to be more nurturing toward their children and partner. All this machismo is causing them to miss out on enriching, bonding experiences with the members of their families, and that's simply not healthy for anyone involved.

People, we are failing each other. We are creating an environment in which everybody is just surviving, and nobody is thriving.

So how can we change the future outcomes for ourselves, our men, and our kids? How can we create equitable environments at home and at work so that everyone can thrive?

Here's What Moms Can Do

- Stop gatekeeping.

- Make space for dads to do more (by doing less).

- Be honest about the realities of motherhood to expand people's understanding of the experience.

- Accept help from friends and loved ones.

- When able, offer help to friends and loved ones.

- Partake in historically "male" tasks (fixing things around the house, yardwork, grilling, etc.) and encourage your partner to explore historically "female" tasks (household cleaning, cooking, caretaking, etc.); sometimes to see a change, you have to be the change.

Here's What Dads Can Do

- Take advantage of parental leave.

- Stop believing that women do the majority of care work because we want to ('cause we don't).

- Ensure leisure time is afforded to their baby mamas. (Studies show that people who have more leisure time and time for creative activities tend to perform better at work.)

- Derive self-worth not only from their job but also from how well they raise their kids.

- Stand up for the women in their workplace—call out biases and stop harassment when they witness it.

- Police themselves when teaching their kids about the roles of men and women in society.

- Become positive role models for other men by showing that caring for themselves and the well-being of others is a human trait, not just a feminine trait.

Here's What Society Can Do

- Value caregiving and child raising more; after all, it is how we shape the future of society and this planet.

- Implement paid leave policies that provide both maternity and paternity leave.

- Ensure paternity leave is non-transferable so that men are more likely to take advantage of it, reducing the gender differences in labour force participation rates.

- Reduce gender stereotyping in childcare and related household responsibilities.

- Stop rewarding men financially when they become dads and punishing women financially when they become moms.

- Quantify the value of unpaid domestic work.

- Embrace transparency surrounding salaries: The gender pay gap can only survive in a culture of secrecy.

- Embrace flexibility in work schedules so that the corporate world can become more inclusive.

- Use the taxation system to create incentives for caring work by men (for the sick, for elders, and for children) and incentives for equality in family life.

- Disincentivize employers to demand overtime work, and delineate a legal structure for permanent part-time work (and incentivize men to use it).

A SMALL VICTORY: GENDER EQUITY

By Nikita Stanley

I had my first son when I was 25. He was not planned; I was not married. My partner and I (still not married, for the record) spent the majority of the pregnancy scrambling to sell our tiny condo and buy a slightly less tiny house to raise our little family in. By the time we got settled, we had only a few months to get things organized for the big arrival; amid the excitement and chaos (compounded with our youth and naïveté), planning for equitable workload sharing simply never happened.

That was back in 2014, when parental leave among dads was still considered taboo and there was no Rebel Mama around to state otherwise, so lo and behold, I gave birth and my partner and I fell directly into our prescribed gender roles. He went to work, made money, and dealt with the finances. I stayed at home, maintained our joint investment (the house), contributed a portion of my halved salary to our expenses, and kept the baby (and dog) alive.

I went back to work part-time after a year of mat leave, only to find myself pregnant with baby number two soon thereafter. Once again, I was back in domestic territory—this time with a two-year-old, an infant, and a budding business in tow.

I never did go "back to work" after that. Instead, I articulated my goals and crowdfunded them, thereby creating a job for myself that would allow me the freedom to design my schedule around my needs and those of my family. It was a risk, but one that I was willing to take—mostly because by then I was 100 percent committed to the Rebel Mama dream of smashing stigmas and supporting new moms through their transition into parenthood. Right around that time, my partner—the saint that he is—decided to follow his heart to a passion project coaching kids' hockey that quickly snowballed into a second full-time job.

So, for three years we lived in overdrive as our kids and business ventures grew rapidly. We were both hustling really hard. Always rushing from one thing to another, passing each other in the entryway of our home like ships in the night. He was coming home late from practice; I was dashing out to host an event. He was leaving the house at the crack of dawn for work; I was scrambling to get the kids to their respective childcare providers in time to squeeze in five hours of writing, an hour of housework, and 30 minutes of dinner prep before the school day was done.

And then came March 2020. The COVID-19 pandemic made its way to Canada and shut down the whole damn circus that we didn't even realize we'd been performing in.

Like so many families, in a matter of 48 hours, our lives as we'd known them came to a screeching halt. There was no longer anywhere to rush to. Organized sports were cancelled, my partner was told to work from home indefinitely, schools were closed, daycares were closed, and suddenly there we were: One girl, three boys, and a dog named Eddie, together 24/7 in our 1,200-square-foot Toronto row house, forced to figure out a way to coexist while homeschooling, maintaining a clean, happy household, and cooking three fucking meals a day with zero outside help.

There was a silver lining, though, as there always is: We all (yes, even my two young sons) came to realize that our roles within the microcosm of our home were going to have to change. Everyone was going to have to pitch in to ensure the household ran smoothly. We would all have to learn new skills and work collaboratively to not just survive, but thrive. And so just like that—literally overnight—a global pandemic introduced gender equity to our home in a meaningful, tangible way for the first time in our six years together as a family. Go fucking figure.

The curveball here is literally that which you're currently holding in your hands. Yes, friends, this very book was birthed in quarantine. When the world shut down, this book's deadline was the only thing left to rush for. What that meant was, for the first time in the history of my and my partner's relationship as parents, my work skyrocketed to the top of the priority list and household roles had to be urgently reassigned.

Hallelujah!

My partner contacted his employer to explain our situation and landed on a combination of time off and part-time work that allowed him to take on the role of primary caregiver to our kids (now six and four). I was home to give guidance where needed ("Hey, can I wash this red T-shirt with these white sheets?") and cook most household meals (something I generally enjoy), but by and large, Daddy was left to figure out the minutiae and I was left the hell alone.

Being a natural control freak/perfectionist (don't be jealous), I had to remind myself often that many of the skills I'd taken for granted as a tandem power mom and work-from-home business owner are skills that took a lot of time and trial and error to acquire. Removing myself from the situation became important. Not just in the times when I was working (read: locked in our bedroom upstairs) but also in my "leisure time."

For a primary caretaker of children, "leisure time" is an abstract concept—you may be vaguely aware of its existence, but it's not necessarily part of your daily reality. As the "working parent," leisure time really did manifest itself—mostly in lag times between conference calls, when the boys had curled up on the couch to watch a movie or gone out in search of an empty field in which to burn off some quarantine energy. But notwithstanding from whence it sprang forth, I decided to use those fleeting moments to mirror the learning that my partner was doing all day as PIC (parent in charge).

And so I began to teach myself how to do handy work. Unclogging sinks, doing minor landscaping, painting. You name it, I learned it (shout-out to YouTube for the quick and dirty education). I figured that equity is a two-way street, and if my partner was going to learn how to undertake traditionally "female" activities, then I'd better do the same with traditionally "male" ones.

You know what I learned?

Traditionally male work is easy as fuck. Like, it's easier than you could ever imagine. Power tools make it exponentially easier. I highly recommend you school yourself in the art. Not only is it satisfying as hell, but saying "I'm going to change the light bulbs and sand the back porch" also gives your partner the chance to say, "Okay, I've got the kids and will get dinner started." You know what's 50,000x more chill than wrangling kids while pre-paring a meal? Changing light bulbs upstairs and painting shit in the yard. I spent a lot of my downtime in isolation reading about how pandemics are absolute disasters for feminism. Even as of June 2020, as Canadian provinces began to open, what was the first thing anyone noticed? Markedly low numbers of women returning to their jobs in comparison to men. For those of us who have been fighting for societal gender equity, this is heartbreaking. But when business opens before childcare, what the fuck else did anyone expect to happen?

But I digress. I'd love to sign off with a neat "happily ever after" but the truth is, I don't know how this story ends. All I can offer you are the strange and glorious pandemic lessons I internalized in 2020, and they are as follows:

1. Kids learn more from our example than our words. When you're busy, sometimes you don't even realize what values you're modelling and perpetuating in your own home. Slowing down allows us to be more deliberate about what we're teaching our kids with our actions.

2. As women, undertaking traditionally masculine tasks liberates male partners to undertake traditionally feminine tasks (and can also result in toned biceps and a sweet tan).

3. If you need time to make shit happen, you have to take it. Nobody's going to give it to you.

4. Childcare is vital to societal productivity. Perhaps we shouldn't be paying so damn much for that shit out of pocket.

5. Change begets change. Like a domino effect—once it starts, look out.

COVID-19, with all its fear and uncertainty, brought a necessary change of pace, a change of priorities, and a change of activity for those of us who were privileged enough to weather the storm at home. In my house, it brought a kind of labour equity that I pray we won't lose our grasp on as we pick up the broken pieces of our world and glue them back together. But if history has taught me anything, it is to always remain cautiously hopeful and unwaveringly vigilant in the face of progress. We took one step forward; we must not take two back.

Part 3

SPENDING

Spending is a necessary aspect of every capitalist society.

(We just want to make sure you're doing it wisely.)

CHILDCARE EXPENSES (READ 'EM AND WEEP)

When it comes to spending money, childcare will force you to make it rain like never before. When we ourselves were making the decision about who was going to watch our kids while we re-entered the real world, we were completely blind to the necessity of getting on daycare wait-lists as early as possible—you basically need to be applying for that shit while your baby is still in utero. As a result, we ended up with nannies. We fondly recall the years of full-time in-home *actual help* as some of the best of our lives . . . But we admittedly made this decision without really understanding the breadth of the options available to us because we were too busy worrying about keeping the baby alive to dedicate large blocks of time to research.

If you're interested in this chapter there's a good chance that you're either a new mom returning from parental leave or you're a veteran mom re-entering the workforce; either way you're probably dying at the thought of adding *another* thing to your list of shit to figure out. Don't worry, that's why we're here, babe. We did the research for you so that you could see all the options available to you before making this fiscally and emotionally important decision. You're welcome.

Daycare

If you're thinking of sending your kid(s) to daycare, you're going to have to play a good long game. That's because wait-lists for daycare centres in Canada are absolutely insane. But if you do your homework early (like, really early . . . like, conception early), you'll be able to reap the numerous daycare benefits of regular schedules, age-appropriate activities, and socialization time with peers and other adults. While choosing a daycare may be a nerve-racking experience for many parents, finding one in which children are supported, engaged, and encouraged can be a total gamechanger in the overall happiness of every member of the family.

The Cost

There are three categories of daycare:

- **Infant:** birth to 24 months

- **Toddler:** 18 months to 36 months

- **Preschooler:** 30 months to kindergarten age

The prices associated with full-time care in each category vary widely, with infants' spots being most expensive thanks to high demand/low supply. The silver lining, however, is that as your kid moves up through the ranks, your childcare bills will go down. Bless.

Costs also vary (*a lot*) from province to province.

David Macdonald and Martha Friendly's 2017 "Time Out" study found that the top three Canadian cities with the highest childcare costs are located in the Greater Toronto Area:

> Toronto is the most expensive city for childcare, with the median cost of full-time infant care in the city being $1,758 a month, or $21,096 annually. Second highest was Mississauga (ON), where parents pay at the median $1,452 a month, followed closely by another Greater Toronto Area (GTA) city, Vaughan (ON), with median fees of $1,415.

Ready for a real kick in the pants? Guess what the infant fees are in Montreal.

Lower . . .

Lower . . .

Lower . . .

Alright, you'll never guess.

$168 a month! That's 10 times cheaper than Toronto! *kill us now* So what gives?

Well, Quebec, Manitoba, and PEI all got their $hit together and opted to pay childcare operation costs, thereby allowing them to set more affordable maximum childcare fees provincially. Must be nice.

Wait! you may be thinking. *Didn't you say that toddler and preschool care is cheaper?*

Yes—a little. In Toronto, you're looking at $1,354 and $1,150, respectively.

It's important to note that people living in rural communities—even in hella expensive Ontario—take a much more moderate hit to the old pocketbook. In rural southwestern Ontario, for example, you're looking at only $781 per month for preschool fees.

What's clear is that when it comes to the price of childcare in Canada, three things matter most: location, location, location. If you're family planning, don't underestimate the impact of your postal code on your expenses.

Nanny

Nannies are a favourite childcare option for many working parents. Why? Convenience, baby! You dictate the schedule and set the ground rules. They help you keep the house in order, aid in meal prep, and generally give you peace of mind knowing that you've got an extra set of hands on deck on the home front. And if you're worried about socialization, you can sign them up for local neighbourhood meetups to ensure your kid squeezes in a little play time with other kids every day—bada bing, bada boom.

If you have one kid, a nanny will cost more than daycare, but if you have two or more rug rats requiring care, it's actually the more economical option (daycare doesn't give a break on subsequent enrollments—sweet, right?). Keep in mind, though, that not all nannies are comfortable with handling twins or multiple children, so paying your nanny extra (still not nearly as much as double the daycare) to look after more kids makes you an attractive employer.

The downside of hiring a nanny is that payment is a bit more complicated than a set daycare fee. You're hiring an employee. That requires research, interviewing, negotiation, and, once you've chosen "the one" it also requires an understanding of tax obligations and other deductions that you're responsible for. But let's start with the hard costs.

The Cost

The cost of hiring a nanny can vary widely depending on your area and family type. While some nannies are paid minimum wage, others have a starting pay of $20 per hour—so it is best to take into consideration all aspects of what you are looking for in a nanny before settling on a salary. For example, do you expect the house to be cleaned? Laundry done? Meals prepped? Those are all reasonable requests, so long as they're accompanied by fair pay, of course. Note that when you're discussing wages with your nanny, it is best to talk in terms of gross pay rather than net pay. The gross pay amount is closer to what's going to come out of your pocket; the net pay is what goes into your nanny's pocket.

According to data collected by Canadiannanny.ca, in 2018, the average nanny charged $17.09 per hour, with anything between $15 to $19 being common. On the higher end, nannies charged $22.35 per hour. On the lower end, $12.72 per hour.

In Canada, wage averages can vary between cities and even within neighbourhoods. Ask friends, join a parent/nanny group on Facebook, or ask your neighbours what they have paid in the past and use that as a rough benchmark, but always take your provincial minimum wage into consideration, too.

Some other things to keep in mind when hiring:

- Not every nanny is comfortable with every age group.

- More years of experience will also lead to higher pay, simply because a more experienced nanny can provide a higher-quality level of care for your child.

- If a nanny works for a family for an extended period, it is common for them to receive a raise.

Live-Out vs. Live-In

In larger cities such as Toronto, Vancouver, or Calgary, a live-out nanny typically charges between $14 and $20 per hour. In rural areas, nannies often cost less (just like rural daycares). Live-out nannies need to have clearly defined hours and days each week to accurately calculate pay. If they end up working longer hours than you agreed on, it's on you to provide overtime pay.

The wage of a live-in nanny in Canada ranges between the minimum wage and $15 per hour.

In rural communities, the rates tend to be lower for live-in nannies as well. With live-in nannies, the boundaries of clearly defined hours can get a little blurred. In this case, you'll want to ask yourself the following before determining pay: Will the nanny have to be on call during all hours of the day? What type of household chores will be expected of them? When are their guaranteed off-hours? Remember, the more time you want your nanny to be available, the higher their rate should be.

Household Tasks

Since kids do not require full attention 24/7, it's common for families to ask their nannies to perform some tasks on the side in addition to childcare. The most common ones are light housekeeping and meal prep. Some nannies will gladly take on the responsibilities; others will not. It's best to be upfront about your expectations during the interview process and be ready to pay more with each task you add to the list.

Families looking for live-in nannies should be especially clear about expectations.

CPP, EI, and Other Deductions

In addition to your nanny's gross pay, there are some other costs that you'll want to be aware of, namely: employer contributions to Canada Pension Plan (CPP) and Employment Insurance (EI). These, plus tax deductions (and room and board in the case of live-in caretakers), should be accounted for in your nanny's gross pay amount. To make your life easy, go ahead and open a payroll account online to ensure you provide your nanny with accurate pay and pay stubs for each pay period. Your accountant and your overall sanity will thank you.

If the costs seem too high, but you still need flexible childcare in a hurry, you may consider a **nanny share** arrangement with someone in your neighbourhood. A nanny share is when one nanny cares for children from two different families at the same time. Although this kind of goes without saying, you'll want to make sure you *actually like* the family with whom you're buddying up. Be clear about the number of hours you require, and discuss whether or not you'll split time between homes or choose a hub (remember: baby gear is really annoying to lug around, so sometimes keeping the caregiving in one home works out better for everyone involved).

If you're ready to start the journey to shared nanny-hood with a trusted friend or neighbour, make sure to carve out some time to discuss everyone's expectations pertaining to (a) cleaning duties, (b) scheduling specifics, (c) the term of the agreement (it may be a good idea to schedule a parent "check-in" every three to six months to ensure everyone is still happy), and (d) shared rules/parenting styles. A nanny share can really be the best of both worlds—early socialization *and* convenience, plus each family saves significantly on childcare expenses while the nanny enjoys higher pay than they would with the typical full-time position. Everybody wins. But do yourself a favour and have a basic agreement in place before you embark upon this journey together; this is a relationship you want built on a strong foundation. Communication will be key.

Au Pair

If you have a bit of extra space in your home, you don't require full-time assistance, and you like the idea of giving a youngster from a foreign country the Great Canadian Child Rearing Experience, then an au pair might just be the childcare option for you. The wait time is tolerable (generally between four and eight weeks), the wages are manageable (think minimum wage, minus room and board), and if you play your cards right, you can even arrange some evening hours so you can reclaim a small piece of that roaring social life you used to pride yourself on.

An au pair is a young person (typically a young woman) who takes care of your children and does light housekeeping for up to 12 months. Au pairs come from around the world but mainly from Australia, New Zealand, Mexico, Germany, and the UK. They expose your family to other cultures, languages, and customs without requiring transcontinental air travel with the whole fam. Score!

The term *au pair* is French and means "equal to," implying that the relationship between you, your children, and your au pair is both reciprocal and respectful. An au pair works 25 to 30 hours per week according to your needs. They do not work full-time like a live-in caregiver does.

The best way to find an au pair is through a reputable agency with a comprehensive screening process. Before your au pair's arrival, they will make sure that (a) you're not inviting an escaped convict into your home, (b) you and your au pair are aware of cultural differences, and (c) you have all the info you need to make this year-long commitment work for everyone involved.

As a "host," you are required to provide the au pair with a private, lockable bedroom and a welcoming home environment and that's about it.

The Cost

Au pairs are paid minimum wage (which varies in every province in Canada) and then room and board (which also varies) can be deducted. Pay should reflect the number of children and level of responsibility.

Keep in mind that because of the complicated nature of hiring an au pair, you will likely have to pay an agency a set fee for placement assistance. That fee can vary from $1,000 to $1,500, depending on the au pair's level of expertise and whether you are a returning customer to a particular agency. Once that fee has been cleared, you're looking at an investment of about $250 (part-time) to $500 (full-time) per week.

Household Tasks

An au pair will typically be willing to do household duties related to the children but not those related to you, your pets, or your partner. An au pair is not a housekeeper. They're also likely to be pretty young. How good at cleaning were you when you were 19? That's what we thought.

Babysitter

Hey, remember babysitters? With the prevalence of professional childcare providers and licensed daycare centres, it's easy to forget about the OG. If you're a child of the '80s or '90s, the memories you have in connection to the term *babysitter* likely involve braces with colourful elastics, crimped hair, and tube socks with white runners. Today's babysitters are like those of days past in that they tend to either be

- the most responsible kid in your neighbourhood;

- your relative; or

- your best friend's kid, who needs an intro to adult responsibilities.

Because it's the '20s now, there are apps and services you can use to find a babysitter in a pinch, but we find that people often feel better about leaving their kids in the hands of a questionably qualified teenager with whom they have some kind of rapport.

More often than not, babysitters are hired to cover the evening hours during which mama and papa are going out to get their groove on (or to attend their boss's retirement party, whatever). Generally, they don't prepare food (other than snacks), they don't clean up, and they sure as hell do not do the laundry. A babysitter's job is to put your kid to bed (if you haven't already), and then sit quietly in the living room while the kid slumbers. In exchange for their time, you will pay a fee that you have discussed with them and/or their parents.

The Cost

The lines are a wee bit blurry on this one, but the general rule is to pay your sitter your province's minimum wage x number of hours worked. We've known some families, however, to call it $10/hour plus pizza and an Uber home. Others negotiate a lower rate for simply sitting in the house while the kids sleep and a higher one for times when the kids are awake. No matter the agreement you come to, what's important is that everyone is happy, the sitter feels valued, and you feel comfortable with the person you're leaving in charge during your absence.

Summer Camp

This amazing thing happens when your child enters the school system: free, full-time (almost) childcare, and the immense joy (yours, mostly) that arises from it. The liberation takes your breath away. *Finally*, you have guaranteed time during the day to Get. Shit. Done. And you don't have to pay $1,200 a month for it anymore! Hallelujah!

But then: summer. Suddenly, you've got nine weeks' worth of childcare that need to be accounted for. You can hire a short-term nanny. College/university students on summer holidays are fantastic for this. One summer we had a nanny who had come to Toronto from Boston to study early childhood education and wanted to make a little scratch on the side when she wasn't in school. She was incredible. Hiring her was absolutely the right choice for us at the time. My kids *still* recall it as the best summer ever.

But as the kids get older, city-run camps have started to stand out as the ideal summer childcare option because (a) they're subsidized, so they're definitely the least expensive childcare option out there, and (b) they're fucking awesome! If you live in a Canadian metropolis, chances are the camps available to you are pretty great, too. Our kids have done art camp, sports camp, adventure camp, outdoor adventure camp, and swimming camp—all out of our local recreation centres.

In Toronto, camp enrollment officially starts at age four, but you start to get into more options and programming choices at age six. (There are also camps available for March and winter breaks.)

The only downfall is the insane sign-up process that involves

1. getting set up with a family PIN and a separate code per child (this can be done in person at your local rec centre or over the phone);

2. tracking your sign-up dates like a fucking maniac;

3. getting up before sunrise on sign-up day to secure a spot;

4. having all the codes for the programming you want written down so you're ready to rock 'n' roll as soon as registration opens; and

5. frantically adding codes to your cart (don't worry, once they're in the cart, they're yours, so if you need to purchase multiple weeks of camp, you can just keep on searching and adding to cart, just like you used to on Net-a-Porter).

The Cost

If you're applying for a city-run camp in your neighbourhood, it will cost anywhere from $150 to $200 per week, per child, and entitle you to childcare from 9 a.m. to 4 p.m. If you're applying to a camp outside of your neighbourhood, you'll be charged approximately 10 percent more.

There are nine weeks of summer break for public schools—many of them housing long weekends—so be aware of plans (and possible plans) when signing up (frantically, at seven in the morning).

When you add it all up, paying between $600 and $800 per month for full-time childcare is a walk in the park compared to hiring a nanny to watch your kid for the same amount of time.

So, if you're updating your budget sheet as you go, you'll want to factor in between $1,350 and $1,800 per year (spread over June, July, and August) in full-time summer childcare.

If you want to limit those costs, consider using some vacation time to stay home with the kids and having your partner do the same. Book a cottage for a week or set up some sweet travel plans. See what your family and friends are up, too (and if they want to add your spawn to their escapades)—you never know! Establish your plans early and you'll save yourself a few weeks' worth of camp money.

There is also the option of private summer camps. These can offer some amazing programming, but you can bet your sweet ass that it comes with a hefty price tag.

Hot Guy Break!

Just thinking about childcare is a total bitch—and then there's actually going through the motions.

Here's to you, sis.

ESSENTIALISM (YOUR NEW FAVOURITE WORD)

Get excited because the theory of essentialism is quite simple and can be applied to most aspects in life. As you may have gathered from its name, it is the act of consciously making decisions that are *essential* to your being, your business, and your life. It's about asking yourself, every time, if this decision you are making is aligned with the future you see for yourself. As a society, we've become accustomed to instant gratification—we want it all and we want it now (hence Prime is slaying). But what we really need to do is shift our focus to satisfying our need for the right thing, with the right reason, at the right time. For this to happen, we need to practise patience, be steadfast with our priorities, and constantly ask ourselves: *Is this essential?*

It's all too easy to fall into the trap of fulfilling needs immediately, as doing so produces that awesome serotonin rush and excitement—it's what retailers depend on. But what would happen if you just paused to think?

Take the hypothetical new sofa you desperately "need" in your life right now.

Do you need it because you saw a sponsored ad on Instagram 10 minutes after you uttered the words? Is your current sofa completely hopeless? Can it be reupholstered for the time being? Can the purchase wait until you find the right piece, for the right price? Is it an *essential* spend right now? Chances are, unless you literally do not have a place to sit, you don't *need* the damn sofa. Also, it's fair to note here that if you have small children residing at your home, said sofa would likely get vomit, pee, and milk spilled on it anyway . . . so you can go ahead and factor that in as well.

Rethinking decisions in this way will not only prove beneficial to your home-life budgeting woes, but when it's applied to business-life, it can really refocus and streamline a lot of your workload and stress. Sometimes (okay, most times) we try to do it all and wonder why we can't get anything done. Doesn't it make more sense to pour energy into only the things that are at the top of the priority list? Get comfortable saying no to things that don't suit. It'll save everyone's time.

Bonus: By taking a pause before mindlessly spending, you'll end up with less, and a clutter-free home plus a clutter-free life (and the mental and physical space that comes with it) is the highest luxury.

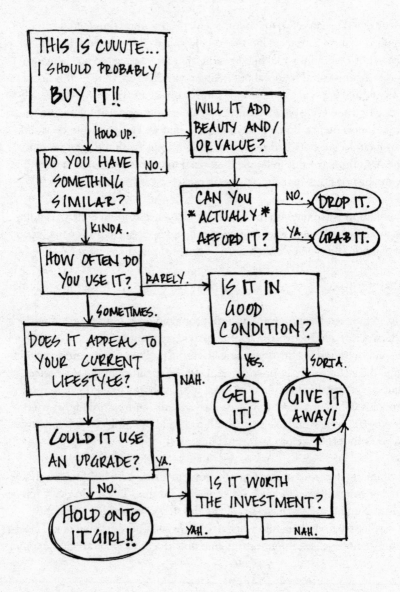

MINDFUL CONSUMERISM (AND WHAT THE HELL IT EVEN MEANS)

In an ideal world, you'll have a few pennies to knock together after paying your monthly living and childcare expenses.

On top of food and shelter, kids do require a fair amount of stuff (clothes, shoes, sporting equipment, books, toys, etc.), but how we buy that stuff is totally up to us as consumers.

Now more than ever, we must take a really hard look at what exactly we're buying, what consequences come with our purchases, and whether we can make better everyday decisions. Although the whole concept of mindful consumerism is admirable, it's no easy feat as the market encourages us to acquire as much as we humanly can, all while making products more disposable and easier than ever to purchase for delivery to your doorstep.

Take "fast fashion," for example. Every season, huge fashion retailers roll out fashion must-haves (read: designer knock-offs) and consumers mindlessly and impulsively add piles of them to their carts. *It's so cheap! It's so easy! I need to have it!* But what is happening on the other end of that transaction is underpaid workers, harmful chemicals, animal abuse, and environmental harm. Not to mention that by the time that same season rolls around next year, your garment will likely be coming apart at the seams and need to be replaced.

So before you purchase your next item du jour, consider these questions:

How often will you use the thing?

This is where one of our favourite math equations comes into play: cost per use. The idea is that the value of an item is directly related to how much use you get out of it. What a novel idea! Now let's put it to work. A well-made pair of $200 jeans may seem like a splurge, but if you wear them three times a week for a year, you're looking at about $1.38 per wear, and we know those babies are going to last years longer than $50 jeans from a discount retailer, which will inevitably stretch out and fall apart. If you're smart with what you need, and take a little extra time doing your research, your purchases will become investments and you will build a collection of essentials that you can rotate until the end of time (okay, maybe not until the end of time—for many good years anyway).

How long will the thing last?

If you know you'll be replacing it sooner than later, a higher ticket price will be the smarter play as it'll cost less in the long run. Good materials age better, so time will only add character to your purchase. Instead of buying a shitty briefcase every two years, aim to buy one solid one every 10.

Can the thing be a vintage/consignment purchase?

Especially in the area of clothing, accessories, and shoes, ask yourself if the thing you need (a winter coat, a Gucci bag, a pair of motorcycle boots) can be purchased from the slew of incredible curated vintage and consignment stores. Not only will the price tag be a lot lower (especially for designer consignment), but you can bet your ass it will be made better, and you don't run the very real risk of showing up to a baby shower in the same Zara floral dress as two other ladies are wearing. *The horror.*

Can the thing be a hand-me-down?

Trade forums and apps are on the rise with good reason. If you're on a budget or need something temporary (read: a baby bouncer for two months), then chances are there's someone out there ready and willing to offload their stuff. In most cases, it's barely used. Even if it does seem well-loved, there are "stroller spas" now that will deep clean the shit out of pre-used gear. P.S. you are not above this—there's nothing "gross" about previously owned items.

What this looks like in real life:

Smart Purchases	Stupid Purchases
Water filter	Cases of bottled water
Only the skin care, makeup, and hair care that you need	Every shiny new bottle you come face to face with at the beauty counter
Well-made vintage furniture	Cardboard furniture
Farmers' market produce	Produce in unnecessary plastic packaging
Reusable coffee cup	Daily coffee runs
If you're in an urban city, a public transit pass or a rideshare app	A gas-guzzling car that costs $30 to park every GD time

If you're a parent, you are likely very well aware of the ridiculous dark holes of mindless spending. It can be easy to get caught up in the desires of ourselves and our children (however valid they may seem at the time), and many parents strive to give their offspring the things they didn't have. It's a sweet sentiment and all, but modelling mindful consumerism in the home is far more beneficial in the long run—and we want these little kiddos to be smart consumers later.

In our first book, *The Rebel Mama's Handbook for (Cool) Moms*, we broke down the things you truly need when baby arrives vs. the slew of shit you definitely do not, and we'd like to continue building that out as the spawns grow. We hope to help you keep money in your pocket and ensure your kids don't grow up to be entitled douchebags.

Shit Your Kids Don't Need	Shit Your Kids Need
Individual devices	Allotted times to use the family iPad
A massive playroom with storage containers full of discarded toys	Toys they love and use. Everything other than sentimental items can be donated to less fortunate children.
Over-the-top Pinterest birthday parties that cost as much as your monthly mortgage payment	A few family and friends, a store-bought cake, and some colourful balloons. A good rule of thumb here is to invite as many friends as your kid's age. Five years = five kids. (You're welcome.)
Video games on video games on video games	Downtime with you
Four extracurricular activities a week (not including the one they're wait-listed for)	One or two extracurriculars and enough free time to get bored
Top-of-the-line sneakers (be honest: That shit's more for you than for them)	Any sneaker that can make it out of a mud puddle alive will do.
A rec room full of arcade games	A walk around the block, or a movie night in
Things	Experiences. It really is the simple things that matter.

UNDERSTANDING MARKETING ALGORITHMS (AND CONTROLLING WHAT YOU SEE)

By now, you've probably noticed that if you so much as utter the words "I wouldn't mind getting a new toaster" in a group chat, you will be inundated with toaster ads for the next three days on every internet page you visit. This is no coincidence, of course.

Everything you type in chats, everything you search for in Google, and most (if not all) of your online behaviour is tracked and used to (a) show you more of what you like and (b) sell you things based on all the collected data. After all, there's a lot of money invested in understanding consumer psychology and controlling buyer needs/wants.

In the case of social media, algorithms sort posts in your feed based on rele-vancy as opposed to the publish time. So, if you recently went down a rabbit hole of supermodel makeup routines, chances are you'll be seeing a lot of related content next time you open the 'gram, and that may or may not be what you want.

The important thing here is to stay aware as you scroll into the deep abyss of the internet and know that you have control of what you see and how it makes you feel. We want to empower you with the necessary tools to help you avoid falling into the online marketing trap and/or feeling shitty about your own circumstances in comparison to a seemingly rich "style blogger" living it up in a Manhattan penthouse (which may or may not be rented for the photo op).

Your diet is not just what you eat—it's what you watch, what you read, and who you spend time with. If you're striving for a healthier mind, you must rid yourself of all the junk from your diet. Be mindful of how you invest your time. Listen to the voice inside your head; pay attention to how things make you feel. Connect with people and brands that inspire you and reflect your own values, and everything will fall into place.

Your online life needs just as much attention and effort as your real life, and it should be utilized to its maximum potential. And remember, *less* is more here. Choose only those that make the cut.

Quick and Immediate Fixes for a Blissful Online Existence

Mute button: Wouldn't it be nice if it worked IRL? When you come across something/someone annoying AF that has you rolling your eyes immediately, click the Options button (three dots on the top right-hand side) and mute that toxic shit, or simply unfollow if you're ready for a clean break.

Notification settings: When you come across a person/brand that makes you feel the opposite (positive, empowered, curious), go back to those same options and turn notifications on. You will now get the most recent posts as soon as they hit the web and see more related content as a result.

Reporting ads: Sponsored ads that have no business being in your social feeds are weird. *Whaaat? Why am I even getting this ad?!* It's an extra step but reporting them does help the app learn what you definitely are not interested in (and never want to see again), and it cuts down on the ads you see in general.

Unsubscribing: It takes a bit of legwork at the beginning, but we urge you to commit to unsubscribing from promo emails as soon as they hit your mailbox. After a while, you will discover the beautiful peace that is receiving only emails you want and need.

Part 4

DEBT

Debt is one of those realities of adult life that you're just going to have to accept. It can be a major source of stress and anxiety, especially when you know you're about to be hit with an uptick in expenses, but remember this: (a) Not all debt is bad, and (b) creating an efficient money-management plan while you're still working on debt repayment is absolutely possible.

STEP ONE: FIND OUT YOUR CREDIT SCORE

Hold on—what even is a "credit score" and how is it calculated?

A credit score is a number between 300 and 900 that reflects how much credit you've had and for how long, and how well you've done paying it off.

Our credit scores took a hit when we had kids and started a business at the same time—but that's literally why credit exists in the first place. Bringing a child into the world is a huge financial blow for any family. And that's okay. If you have to go into savings or rely on credit for a period to survive, you are not alone. Many of us do. And if the prospect of finding out your credit score is bringing up some serious fear, anxiety, or insecurity, just remind yourself that this is simply the first (and arguably most important) step of finding out where you are now so you can navigate toward where you want to go from here.

Now take a deep breath and head on over to either transunion.com or equifax.ca, give them the cash equivalent of three oat milk lattes, and in return they will allow you a peek at your score.

Once you get it back, here's how to decode it:

The more likely you are to default on a loan, the closer to 300 your score will be. This means that if you *do* get a loan, you will have to pay a higher interest rate to make up for your riskiness.

The less likely you are to default on a loan, the closer to 900 your score will be. In that case, if you were to get a loan, you would be rewarded for your trustworthiness with a lower interest rate.

The higher the score, the more power you'll have in situations where you need to play hardball with the bank—like, for example, when you're buying a home or opening a business. You would be surprised how quickly interest rates can change and monthly service charges are waived when you let them know *you* know your worth.

So, what constitutes a "good" credit score?

Strive for at least 700. Some say that any score from 660 to 725 is considered "good," 725 to 760 is "very good," and the highest scores (760 to 900) are considered "excellent." Scores from 560 to 659 put you in the "fair" credit category, likely making lenders consider you "high risk." (Anything under 559 is poor.) If you're even able to get credit, you'll probably pay a higher interest rate than someone with a score that's just 20 or 30 points above yours.

Think of the world as a fancy Vegas hotel: Your credit score is the key to the deluxe suite. A good credit score will give you VIP access to better rates and terms if you require quick credit down the line. It also affects what card offers you get, what deposit utilities require, what your insurance rate will be, whether you get that rental apartment, or what your installment plan is for a cellphone. In our society, it's a three-digit number that can open or shut doors.

STEP TWO: IMPROVE YOUR CREDIT SCORE

So how can you get a good credit score or improve a shitty one? There is no magic formula—well, there is, but sadly it's not available to the general public. Credit score calculations themselves are proprietary, meaning that, besides the agencies, no one knows exactly how they're done. But we do know the factors that companies like TransUnion and Equifax take into account when coming up with a score, and that is often all we need to take action. If your goal is to improve your credit score, then ask yourself: Do I pay my bills on time? How much credit do I use vs. what's available to me? Did I take on more debt recently?

Also keep in mind that having a long-established credit history is key to building a good credit score, which means that older people will generally have higher credit scores than their younger counterparts (#agebefore-beauty). Don't worry too much about that, though, because the biggest factor in calculating your credit score is paying bills on time, which is totally within your control (and if your memory sucks as much as ours, automation is your friend!).

Staying considerably below your credit limit on each credit card makes a difference, too, as does spreading out balances between more than one card. As for improving a not-so-great score, there's no quick fix, but here are some extra tips from Wealthsimple to get you started:

1. **Check for credit report mistakes:** Order your credit report from one of the sites listed above to ensure it only includes accurate information. You can order a credit report for free once a year from them. A credit report is not a score, but it contains the information used to calculate a score. It's a document several pages long that contains your personal information like your SIN, address, and credit payment history; any collections, judgments, or bankruptcies; and a list of lenders that have recently asked about your credit. You'd be surprised at the potential for mistakes and oversights.

While it may first appear that credit agencies are government regulated or owned, they are not. They are private businesses working on behalf of lenders to help determine the risk level of borrowers. And just like any other organization, they make plenty of mistakes. Note that mistakes can also be a sign that someone is trying to steal your identity, so it's always good to keep an eye on it.

Contact both the lender and credit bureau about any errors, and they will investigate your claim. If you're not satisfied with the result, then you can escalate your case and add a note to your file explaining your side of the story. If necessary, you can also file a claim with the Office of Consumer Affairs.

2. **Pay your debt on time:** By far the most important thing you can do to increase your credit score is to pay your bills, specifically your *debt*, on time. Remember this: It's better to pay the minimum interest of your debt on time than to pay the debt off in full a week late.

If this is (or if you foresee it will be) an issue for you, then consider setting up automatic payments with your bank. It may also help to schedule an hour once a month to sit down and look at all your bills and assess your debts.

If you need to dispute a bill, then contact your lender, but still pay the minimum payment required for now.

3. **Don't be too eager when paying off debt:** It's okay to carry *a little* debt. While it is commendable, and personally responsible, to pay off all your debt every single month, we must remember that lenders actually make money off your debt. The best kind of borrower (in their eyes) is one that racks up interest and pays it in a timely manner, not necessarily one that racks up debt and pays it before any interest is charged.

Visa and Mastercard, for example, don't make any money off you when you pay your balance in full every month. They only make money when you remain in debt and pay interest. So, while we definitely don't recommend purposefully staying deep in debt, it's also okay to find a debt repayment plan that fits within your budget, instead of going crazy trying to live on boiled cabbage just to pay off every last dollar of your bill this month.

4. **Take on various forms of debt once you are able to trust yourself to pay it all back on time:** Lenders like to see variety—a credit card, a line of credit, a car loan. Different forms of debt show lenders that you can handle repayment well.

Boosting your credit score will happen naturally with time as you become a better borrower. And being a better borrower includes only taking on debt that you know you can pay back in full in an appropriate amount of time. OBV don't start taking on more debt if you can't handle the debt you have now. Only start adding different kinds of debt if you can trust yourself to pay it all back on time.

5. **Keep your old credit cards:** Don't bother cancelling a credit card before it expires. Cut it up and throw it in the trash instead. Cancelling a card will delete part of your credit history, and as we know, a long credit history helps you improves your score.

6. **Don't constantly take on new credit:** It's not a good idea to constantly take on new credit. If you need to borrow more, consider paying down your current balance to free up room.

Lenders view it suspiciously if every week you're going from store to store, or bank to bank opening new credit cards. It's okay to take on additional or diverse kinds of debt as long as it's not too frequently and as long as you don't actually use it all (see point 4).

Keep in mind that every time you apply for debt, it shows up on your credit report and will temporarily drag down your score.

7. **Limit hard credit checks:** A hard credit card check is when a lender requests your credit history to determine if they want to advance you money. Anytime you apply for a credit card, a job, an apartment, or a mortgage, it's possible that the lender will perform this credit check. Sometimes it's unavoidable and the effects are only temporary anyway. Reduce hard checks by only applying for more credit when you really need it. Also, consider asking a landlord if they will accept a screencap or printout of your credit score instead. Checking your own credit score does not affect it in any way, and you can do so for 15 bucks online.

The takeaway here: Improving your credit score will happen naturally as you become a better borrower. Every month is a new opportunity for you to prove that you're someone lenders want to give credit to. Developing good financial habits and maintaining those habits over time is the best way to improve your credit score.

Here's how the Credit Slice divvies up:

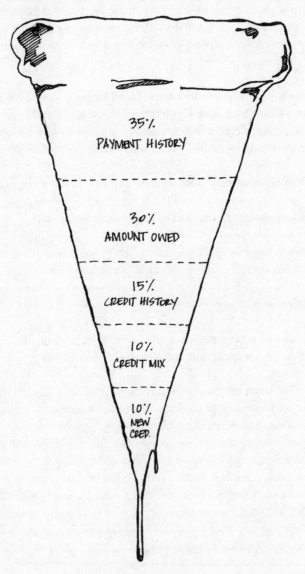

STEP THREE:
FIGURE OUT YOUR
DEBT-TO-INCOME RATIO

Let's dive a bit further into the diagnosis, shall we? In order to do that, it may be useful to figure out your debt-to-income ratio.

According to Wealthsimple, "Your debt-to-income ratio is a metric that explains how much of your income is used to service your debts. Lenders use the debt-to-income ratio to determine if you're in a good financial position to borrow more money," but you can use it, too—to gauge the health of your own financial situation. In other words, use "the system" in your favour, to assist in your personal gains. Don't you just love accounting?

So, how do you calculate your debt-to-income ratio? You simply add up all your monthly obligations (including all sources of debt) and divide them by your total monthly income.

Try it, babe!

Total monthly expenses: _____

divided by

Total monthly income: _____

equals

Debt-to-income ratio: _____

(x 100 to get a percentage)

Now, what qualifies as a "good" debt-to-income ratio?

If you're using this number strictly to assess where you stand in terms of financial health, then whether your ratio is "good" or "bad" is totally subjective. Perhaps a better question to ask: What do the banks consider to be a good debt-to-income ratio? Here's what the pros at Wealthsimple advise:

35 percent or less: This is the safe zone. It means that you most likely have money each month after you pay your bills for living expenses and emergencies. It also means you can probably take on additional debt at a moment's notice for *serious* emergencies and not pay crazy interest rates on it.

36 to 49 percent: If you fall into this bracket, you have room to improve. You're going to want to develop a strategy to lower your debt-to-income ratio so you'll have more wiggle room to handle unforeseen circumstances. The last thing you want is loan-application drama during a time of need.

50 percent or more: Danger Zone. This means more than half of your income goes to debt. After your living expenses, you won't have much to protect yourself from sudden costs. Lenders will limit your borrowing, charge large fees to compensate them for risk, or deny you outright.

If completing this exercise has made you realize that it is high time to get your $hit together and your debt under control, congratulations! You've just taken a step toward financial freedom. Doesn't it feel good?

Now, let's get you out of this shit.

STEP FOUR: IMPROVE YOUR DEBT-TO-INCOME RATIO

There are two ways to improve a debt-to-income ratio (read: get out of debt): (a) reduce your debts, or (b) increase your income.

If you want to give the first option a go, we recommend employing one of the following two debt-busting strategies:

The Debt Snowball

Ideal for people who need some small wins right off the bat to motivate them to keep going

1. Make a list of all debts owing, including the full amount and interest rate.

2. Prioritize them in order of lowest balance to highest balance.

3. Identify and cut out some unnecessary expenses from your life. (That budget you made earlier will be helpful in this activity.)

4. Take the money you've scraped off from limiting unnecessary expenses, and start putting it toward your lowest-balance debt first. Keep paying the minimums on all other sources of debt. Use as many automated tools as possible in doing so (auto-payments are your friend—set them up online or with a teller if you must).

5. Once you've paid off the first block of debt, take the money you were putting toward it and shift it to the next one.

OR

The Debt Avalanche

Ideal for people who are less concerned with small wins and more interested in getting debt-free ASAP

1. Make a list of all debts owing, including the full amount and interest rate.

2. Prioritize them in order of highest interest rate to lowest.

3. Identify and cut out some unnecessary expenses from your life. (Get out that budget again, sister.)

4. Take the money you've scraped off from limiting unnecessary expenses and start putting it toward your highest-interest debt first. Keep paying the minimums on all other sources of debt. Use as many automated tools as possible in doing so (auto-payments are your friend here, too).

5. Once you've paid off the highest-interest debt, take the money you were putting toward it and shift it to the next one. Keep paying minimums on everything else.

Keep the debt repayment train going until you no longer owe anyone shit. Once you're debt-free (hallelujah!), you can really start to invest more for the future.

Pro Tips

• If you've been a responsible account owner, call your lenders and request lower interest rates. You'd be shocked at how quickly they'll jump to reduce your rate to keep your business. If your credit lenders won't reduce your rates (your credit score may be to blame), consider transferring your balances to a 0 percent or low-interest card.

• If you have a lot of loan accounts, consolidate them into a single loan with a lower monthly payment. Yes, smaller monthly payments usually mean *more* total payments, which may affect how much you pay in total, but if you're taking the money you're saving and investing it strategically in your RRSP or TFSA, then you're way ahead of the game.

- *Stop* taking on new debt! Not even those gorgeous Gianvito Rossi heels are worth the headache. Do not make purchases on your credit cards, and avoid taking out any new loans.

We never said any of this would be easy, by the way. But, trust us, it will certainly be worth it. As a major bonus for all the hard work you've put into ditching your debt, you'll automatically receive *an improved credit score!* Yes, girl! With every strategic move you make in paying down debts, you're setting Future You up for success.

Hot Girl Break!

#homagad, credit scores and debt management are so boring. Enjoy the visual therapy.

HOUSEHOLD INVESTMENTS

Home ownership. At first, it may sound romantic, but anyone who has actually made the leap of faith and handed over their life's savings to lock down a home of their own realizes real quick how much work it'll take to maintain it. The furnace is acting crazy. The squirrels are living in the roof. The basement just flooded. The yard is overgrown. And so on and so forth until the end of time, bye.

The positive, quite obviously, is that home improvements equal an increase in home value, and we're all about that kind of math. If you plan properly, the 10 years you spend at this location can also be used toward fixing it up strategically so that, when the time comes, you can sell that shit and make some solid coin.

Always keep in mind, though, that the housing market is volatile, so don't count on your house being your only retirement investment. Your home should be your home. Technically, it is a liability, not an asset (more on that on page 183), so while you could stand to make some cash when you sell, nothing is guaranteed. Make sure you've made some other smart investments in your portfolio while maximizing your home reno effects.

What's Worth Doing in Your Home	Why
Busting down a few walls	You'll gain light and open space (and it'll feel bigger).
Taking the drywall/plaster off your ceiling	You'll grab some extra height, and if it's an old home, you may love the look of what you find underneath.
Demoing tiny closets	Replace them with armoires that you'll love forever and that don't take nearly as much space.
Kitchen and bathroom	When it comes time to sell, they're usually the almighty deal breakers. Countertops, hardware, flooring, tile work, a new sink, wall mirrors—make that shit sparkle and shine.
Small touch-ups	Re-caulking a bathroom or re-staining the cabinets is basically the equivalent of home Botox. A little goes a long way.
The attic	Most people will automatically plan to redo the basement first, but a well-done attic offers natural light and the kind of atmosphere a basement never could.
The basement	Alright, your top floor is fine. Renovating a basement is a great way to make your property earn money if you can squeeze in a bathroom and separate entrance. It also works great as a nanny suite, private guest room, office, or rec room.
Replacing windows and frames	Not only is this an instant facelift, but it will also save you dollars in heating and a/c bills.
Maintaining that curb appeal	By simply updating your front door (black is most en vogue ATM) and your home numbers, you stand to make back a prettier penny when it comes time to sell.

Can't afford a full-on home? Don't worry, you're not alone. Given the current market, most people (especially those residing in large urban cities) are living in townhomes and condos. And honestly, with amenities and property management, it's a pretty sweet set-up.

What's Worth Doing in Your Condo	Why
Flooring	A sleek floor adds a lot of aesthetic value—especially wide plank hardwood. Note: Unless you plan on Swiffering on the daily, don't go with dark floors; instead, aim for a lighter tone to make the room feel more spacious.
Updating appliances	Replacing tired, outdated appliances with stainless steel will make for a glossy feel. If you have extra coin, consider integrating your appliances for a complete look.
Smart storage	Design your own smart storage system with Ikea on the low end, or look into custom work if you're really flush. Either way, it's a win.
Window coverings	Keep it classy and go for a clean blackout roller in a neutral colour. And if you're tempted to go electronic, go with a reputable brand as these can have tech difficulties at times.
Bathroom tiling	Have fun here. It's one of the perks of having a smaller space—a funky wallpaper or marble sink is achievable.
Easy add-ons	Create neat storage under the sink in your kitchen and bathroom(s) to keep all those plastic cleaners, lotions, and potions under control.

Notes from the Wolf (a.k.a. Realtor Marianna Iordanova)

When it comes to the renovations, talk to your agent (who will most likely be reselling the property) and ask what makes the most sense for your dwelling. It's not a one-size-fits-all approach.

Understand that certain renovations will be very personal to you, and you may not get back the same cash you invested when the time comes to sell. You have to decide if you'll be alright with renos that are done solely for your own enjoyment. Personalization can alienate buyers, so be conscious of that.

Do the proper research when hiring contractors. If someone refers a contractor, ask them point-blank if they get a kickback for the lead. It will startle people at first, but this may help gauge how reliable this info is. Also, don't be guilted into using family/friends unless they truly are good at what they do.

Has your property value appreciated since you moved in? A home equity line of credit is the most popular financial tool for renovations, and you can control the rate and payments on it.

Tackle one thing at a time—this year, do a bathroom; next year, do the kitchen. This will likely be more palatable to your financial situation and will give you the time to live in your home long enough to understand exactly what it needs.

Leave it to the professionals. Watching the whole last season of HGTV's *Love It or List It* or a 20-minute YouTube tutorial does not qualify you to barge into your home with a sledgehammer and start demolishing the walls.

Home Economics

Bear with us a moment while we channel our inner octogenarian grandmas and inform you that you (and your partner) are going to have to start maintaining a clean and tidy home. Like it or not, it is your *joint* responsibility to maintain the things you own (or rent), and when it comes to your home, there are two ways to do that: You can either (a) outsource for the going rate of $15–$25 per hour or (b) do it your damn selves. We strongly encourage you to decide together with your cohabitant which suits your current circumstances best. You'll both want to be involved in the duties. (Equity: So hot right now.)

A clean space helps keep your mind sharp, gives the people living in your home an automatic self-esteem boost, and is good for the value of your property. The only downside is that if you're going the DIY route, it chews up an inordinate amount of time and makes you feel like a maid in your own damn house.

If you won't be outsourcing housekeeping, fear not—it really isn't hard once you get in the groove, and the ROI is huge.

Hot Tips for Organizing

- Design a system that makes the most practical sense.

- Place boot trays at the entry points.

- Use hideaway storage for toys.

- Keep shelving tidy and uncluttered.

- Labels galore for all your boxes.

- Invest in storage: Built-in is ideal, but a certain Swedish company makes some great modular items that also do the trick.

- Rid yourself of packaged goods and use containers for pantry items.

- Edit your home and wardrobes relentlessly.

- Sell what you can and give the rest away to friends and neighbours.

- Ask yourself if the item can be "reinvented" to serve a new purpose.

- Divert as much away from the trash can as possible (but, yes, major degradation means a trip to the bin).

Hot Tips for Tidying

- Don't leave a room empty-handed (take something with you and put it back in its designated "spot").

- If a task is going to take less than 60 seconds, do it immediately.

- Tidy your bed as soon as you get out of it (and teach your kids to do the same).

- Never start cooking in a messy kitchen.

- Teach your kids to fold their clothes as best they can and get them involved in putting laundry away early.

- Always put away toys and activities before starting something new (get your kids into this habit, too).

- Unpack backpacks and bags as soon as you get home.

Hot Tips for Cleaning

- Always clean from the top down and from outside edges in.

- Clean any glass surface that carries light into a room, including windows, doors, and light bulbs. *Everything* looks clean when you do.

- Wipe countertops down often (microfibre cloths and warm water will do the trick).

- Keep a stash of cleaning products in the kitchen and in each bathroom.

- Clean the bathroom vanity daily (a quick wipe) and the shower once a week.

- Keep the shower as dry as possible (get a cheap squeegee or keep a designated towel handy).

- Sweep your outdoor entries to prevent dirt and debris from coming inside.

- Invest in a good vacuum cleaner to avoid fixing and replacing it more often than necessary.

- Save on cleaning products and opt for a healthier home existence by making them yourself (vinegar and water are still the best for a mop job).

Living this way will inherently make you more grateful for the things you have and allow you to get into flow state. It can also be meditative AF. Pop in some noise-cancelling headphones and enjoy nirvana (with a side of increased home value).

Mortgages and Home Ownership

One very common form of debt is a mortgage and if buying a house is on your investment to-do list, then it's a concept you'll want to familiarize yourself with pronto.

So what is a mortgage?

It's basically a loan for a house. A big fucking loan for a house that uses the house itself as collateral, meaning that until the loan is entirely paid off, the creditor providing it has a right to take possession of the property and sell it should you default. Yeah, it's serious shit, but don't worry because with a little help from the finance experts at Wealthsimple (and our real estate guru, Mariana Iordanova), we've compiled the info you'll need to know before diving head first into the scariest contract of your life.

How much do I need for a down payment?

The answer to that depends on a few factors, namely: (a) who you ask for advice, (b) how much money you have, and (c) where you're looking to buy. Finance professionals tend to agree that 20 percent of the selling price of the home is what you should aim to put down in cash. Real estate professionals, however, are likely to suggest a more tailored approach. First-time home buyers or people who want to live in real estate hot spots like Toronto and Vancouver may want to consider buying with a smaller down payment, while keeping some cash working hard in an investment account (like an RRSP or a TSFA). Keep in mind that this may necessitate some kind of loan insurance, but if the condo/house appreciation rate is soaring, it could be worth the expense. No matter what you do, just make sure to take your time to assess your goals, be realistic, and talk to a variety of trusted professionals before making any concrete decisions. Also, go ahead and get a mortgage preapproval before you start shopping so you go into the process with a clear idea of what you're working with (and what your future payments will look like).

Alright, how much is this going to cost me every month?

The 50/30/20 Rule dictates that you should spend 50 percent of your income on "needs," 30 percent on "wants," and 20 percent on savings (you'll learn more about this budgeting technique later). As you know, housing costs constitute a need, so to leave room for other important stuff in this category (like food and transportation), you'll want to aim to spend about 30 percent of your monthly income on housing expenses. In a perfect world, that 30 percent should cover your mortgage principal and interest (or rent) in addition to taxes, utilities, and insurance. Go ahead and throw mobile and online access in there, too. If your housing expenses are blowing past that mark, you may want to consider a cheaper home (read: kiss the city goodbye) or paring down on the "wants" category to remain in your desired area.

Can I get a mortgage if I have other debt?

Yes, you can, but you're going to want to make sure your entire monthly debt load is no more than 40 percent of your gross monthly income. Also keep in mind that your credit score will be taken into account when you apply, and so will that debt-to-income ratio you figured out earlier. Banks don't look favourably on anyone whose total debt exceeds 44 percent of their income.

> ***Hot Tip:*** Before you jump into a major purchase (e.g., a car), ask yourself if you're going to need a mortgage in the not-so-distant future. Exorbitant car payments can kill your debt-to-income ratio and harm your chances for qualifying to take on more debt.

What happens if I default on my mortgage?

Nothing good, sister. You'll want to avoid doing so at all costs. If bad luck befalls you and you don't think you'll be able to make the required payments in a timely fashion, get in touch with your lender ASAP. Hopefully you'll get an empathetic soul on the other line who will work with you and give you some payment extensions until you get back on your feet. The absolute worst-case scenario is you stop paying, the bank initiates a power of sale, you get evicted, and the house gets auctioned off. You might recover a little of what you sunk into the house if the sale brings in more than you owed; if it doesn't (and you don't have mortgage insurance), the lender can even go after your wages. The moral of the story? Pay your mortgage. On time. Every month. If you're not sure you can afford to do that, stick to renting and maximizing other investment/saving channels (more on that soon).

Jesus; that sounds scary. What's the upside of getting a mortgage?

Well, for starters, they allow you to not have to pay 100 percent of the cost of a house up front in order to get some equity in one. Also, they're transferable (in Canada anyway)—meaning that if you move before the term of your mortgage is up, you can simply apply that mortgage to a different house and get an additional loan, should you want to upgrade to a fancier abode.

Well, I've got this house now. What should I do with it?

Sink more money into it, of course! This is what makes a house a liability as opposed to an asset, BTW. It's a big fat cash sucker . . . but if you spend that money right, you may just end up with a sizable return at the end (and a happier lived experience in the meantime).

A SMALL VICTORY: DEBT

By Chef Christine Flynn

Back in 2018 I completed my first "baby debt" spreadsheet. I scanned and sorted every receipt from January to July—a six-month snapshot of what it costs in essentials to have a child, or two.

$1,066.87 on groceries.

$405.38 on formula (I more or less gave up breastfeeding when I went back to work in March).

$201.13 on diapers (I also got gifted some!).

$1,896.00 toward RESPs.

$678.00 on life insurance.

$5,820.00 toward my mortgage.

There are a few variables in there. I ended up purchasing my first home in January of that year (down payment, $50K; closing costs, about $10K) and then promptly gutting it ($40K and counting), so I had some lean times. Lots of rice, lots of sardines, and—this is when you know you're really in a hole—no Wi-Fi for a couple months.

The house I bought in wine country had been on the market for a long time. The first time I looked at it, I'd brought a friend with me to help carry my four-month-old twin daughters. The second time, I just handed Matilda off to the real estate agent while I juggled Piper and looked around. There were some structural issues, a horrifying smell, an abundance of dense floral wallpaper, and, strangely, locks on the outside of all the bedroom doors. But it had good bones, I thought. It was unbelievably cheap.

Just a year and a half earlier, I'd been living in a cute little condo on the waterfront, spending my money on dinners out and getting false eyelashes individually glued on. Now I was buying expired milk from No Frills and splurging on a $15 haircut. It wasn't as if I'd made one very large bad decision to get myself, well, let's call it what it was, fucked. I'd made a series of small bad decisions, mixed with some good ones.

To buy the house, I pulled everything out of my RESPs and then borrowed money. I could have put just 5 percent down, which would have been about $12K, but instead I put down 20 percent to get a lower interest rate and put more equity in the home. Then I went ahead and borrowed more money to fix it.

I don't mean to say I just hired someone to gut it. I did do that, yes, but I also did a lot of the work myself. I stripped wallpaper and spackled walls. I pulled the many layers of carpet off the stairs to the basement. I bought my own caulking gun. I watched a lot of YouTube how-to videos. I started making small good decisions. I leaned into JOMO (the joy of missing out). I stopped hanging out with people who made me feel inadequate. I bought less; I made more. I found new support systems and strengthened friendships that served me. I laid down cardboard over the ripped-up floors so my daughters could practise crawling. I went back to work, and then when I realized that wasn't going to be enough money, I got another job, and another, and another. I became my own business, and I scanned and saved receipts for anything and everything I could write off.

It wasn't an unhappy time, though. It sort of felt like camping. And luckily, I quite enjoy tinned fish. (See my recipe on page 168!)

To be fair, I could have spent more and maybe stressed about money less, but, when it comes to debt, I tend to operate more as an avalanche than a snowball. When I went back to work, I took every opportunity I could to make a little extra here and there, and I made big moves like reconfiguring my mortgage, twice, and rolling credit debt into more manageable payments as part of my mortgage. It was a grind, but it was possible, and as of today I am more or less debt-free outside of a very manageable mortgage, a personal loan that ticks down each month, and the odd extremely large Costco bill that spikes my MasterCard balance—because what kind of superhuman can go in there and *not* buy all the things?

I'm still working on the house. Today, my daughters turn three, and while they (and my two dogs) have done some major damage to the walls, the floors, and my productivity, the house has almost doubled in value while my debt continues to tick down, and then sometimes back up, but always in the right direction overall. I know what amount of debt I feel comfortable with, and I know that sometimes it's worth it to get close to that number so I can invest in, say, a dishwasher or a new sewing machine.

One thing I know is that I sure as hell won't be getting false eyelashes glued on anytime soon. I'm very much alright with that.

Part 5

SAVING

Saving is one of those things that you're going to want to start now, if you didn't do it before. In case it hasn't fully sunk in yet, kids are expensive as fuck, and unless you plan on throwing them into the world of child acting really early (don't), they're going to be revenue negative for the foreseeable future. Do you need to be debt-free before you can think about saving? Nope. A well-thought-out debt repayment plan that allows for a little scratch to be set aside at the end of each month is totally doable. Once you're debt-free, however, saving kicks into high gear, and then the passive income can start to roll in.

Financial freedom is in sight, ladies; can you feel it?

THE WEALTH GAP

* on average, women have saved 90k
  <u>less</u> by retirement age than men.

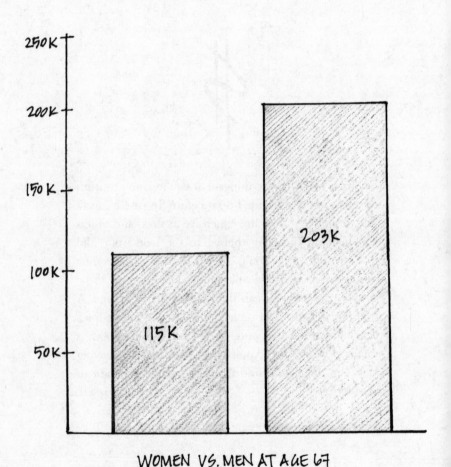

WOMEN VS. MEN AT AGE 67

STRATEGIC SAVING

How much have you got saved up as of now? Statistically speaking, probably not much. It's a well-known fact that, as a demographic, women have far less in savings than men. That's because the savings gap is basically the bridge that connects the wage gap to the wealth gap. Lower wages correlate to lower rates of savings, and lower savings correlate to lower wealth.

All we really want you to take away from this chapter is how important savings can be when it comes to increasing your overall wealth in the long term and getting you through the financial hit of your first few years of parenting in the short term.

Want to take a step toward avoiding the wage gap/savings gap/wealth gap cycle? Then you'll need to curb your desire to spend every penny you make on expensive baby crap that your kid will probably either barf on repeatedly or hate with a fiery passion. As we noted a few pages back, your goal should be to stash 20 percent of your take-home salary to serve all your saving/investing needs. Are these savings going to make you a millionaire before your kid hits kindergarten? No. But they'll help you build up *your own* savings (and, more importantly, establish good saving habits), which will pay off big time down the line. They might even save your ass on a rainy day in your not-so-distant future (e.g., when you realize how much groceries add up to once your kids start on solids or how fun it is when daycare charges you even when you don't use it).

So will beefing up your savings be hard? Probably. Will it be worth it? *Abso-fucking-lutely.*

First order of business is emergency savings. The point is not to put all your eggs in one shitty, interest-earning basket; your goal should simply be to have enough cash handy (in an accessible account) to cover about three months of expenses should unforeseen circumstances prevent you from earning money for a while. Something like, you know, having a baby as a freelancer or being forced to shut down your business during to a global pandemic (COVID-19, what's up!).

So whether this job-dismantling event is anticipated or not, we recommend you make a list of your minimum monthly expenses—the stuff in the "needs" category—and then multiply it by three. Plan to have that magic number of dollars (or more) on hand in case of an emergency.

Why is this little nest egg of yours so important? Because being forced to rely solely on high-interest credit cards for your family's survival is not a scenario you ever want to find yourself in. Those things will suck you drier than that cash-vampire baby of yours!

If you've got a partner whose salary could carry you for a few months, bonus! But you should still put aside some cash, especially if you're working full-time hours. If you don't end up dipping into it after a year, treat yourself by opening an investment account with some of it. Consider it your gift to Future You—that bitch is savvy, and if a good investment opportunity comes her way down the line, she'll thank you for empowering her to act on it.

A word of caution: It's not wise to keep too much of your savings readily available. If you've got more than your minimum safety net in an accessible account, consider moving excess funds to a tax-sheltered investment account where you can really put that coin to work for you (we'll explore that more soon!).

Now that we have you on board with the idea of upping those savings contributions of yours, we should probably serve up some tips to help you do it.

Hot Saving Tips for Parents

- Register strategically. Make sure your friends and relatives know that you give no fucks about keeping up with Pinterest when it comes to your new bundle—you're way too smart to fall into that consumerist trap. Register for the big items that you know you'll need (crib, car seat, stroller, change table), and whatever you don't receive, borrow from friends or buy for next to nothing on the consignment market. If you're dealing with a legitimate consignment company, you'll find the items are cleaned impeccably. Some consignment retailers will even deliver right to your doorstep.

- Don't buy clothing new. Second-hand stores are cool and they are as kind on the planet as they are on your wallet. Heads-up: The stuff you're buying has likely been pre-shrunk by its previous owner, so be safe and size up.

- Shop at the right time of the year. We may not be couponing, but we know when sale season is (for clothing, homeware, travel—all of it). And we know a $500 Christmas tree costs $120 in January, and it already comes in a box ready to shove into the basement.

- Make your own coffee in the morning. At the rates that Americanos go for these days ($3.50 at your favourite hipster café), you're saving almost 20 bucks a week alone. And don't even get us started on artisanal pastry.

- Don't go crazy on expensive extracurricular activities if you can't afford to. There are lots of cost-effective options to keep your elementary schooler occupied through city programs that are often free or very close to it.

- Take it easy on your Uber Eats app. Yes, sometimes it's a total lifesaver and we're all down for pad Thai when you're PMSing, but don't let laziness steer you into overly frequent use, because those delivery charges add the fuck up.

- Automate, baby! Are you really going to leave your brain in charge of reminding you to be responsible and transfer funds to savings every month? Rookie mistake. Use technology to your benefit, and set up automatic transfers so you can focus on forgetting about other stuff instead.

When it comes to saving, the most important tip we can give you is *start now.* You don't have to start with a lot, but the sooner you begin stashing a little cash for later, the better off you'll be in the long run. The reason for that is a little something called compound interest. It's what makes real wealth accruement possible, even when you start seemingly small.

BUDGETING (PHASE TWO)

Here's where that nifty exercise we made you do on page 25 comes back in play. Pull up your budget sheet and start making some edits. You're no longer saving for hospital expenses associated with having a baby or for a nursery. Your kid's heading to school, so a large portion of childcare costs are about to vanish. It's a whole new world, requiring a whole new budget—this time with less shit in the "Expenses" column (kinda). Now it's time to reassess your priorities and establish some new goals. See where you can get creative with your net income, fixed expenses, and variable expenses.

If you keep this budget updated on a monthly basis, track what's working and what's not, make adjustments, and focus on achieving some loftier financial goals, we promise you'll be laughing all the way to bank before you know it.

The 50/30/20 Rule

The 50/30/20 Rule was created as a common-sense tool to assist you in budgeting the money you make (after tax). Here's what it looks like:

- 50 percent of your income is dedicated to "needs," a.k.a. fixed expenses like housing expenses, food, transportation, childcare, and the like.

- 30 percent of your income is allotted for "wants," a.k.a. fun expenses like travel, restaurants, and the hottest footwear of the season.

- 20 percent of your income is set aside to serve your financial goals, including debt reduction, cash savings, and investments.

The idea here is to provide clear spending and saving benchmarks to work toward. You'll want to treat needs and wants as limits (if you have to bend them 5 percent in either direction depending on the cost of living where you are, that's fine) and your savings as a target. Your needs should not account for more than 50 percent of your earnings; if they do, reduce them or figure out how to earn more (read on to learn how). Your wants should not exceed 30 percent of your earnings; if they do, spend less. And if you happen to have saved more than 20 percent, give yourself a pat on the back and consider it an additional win.

Hot Tips for Net Income (and Having More of It)

- Jot down any transferable skills and see if you can manage a side hustle. Even one client a month can add some significant dough to your household. It may also create new opportunities and change your money game completely—you never know.

- Sell your shit. No, really, those AirPods that your family gifted you for your birthday (the ones you never use) run $300 online, and there are plenty of people willing to pay. See what else you can offload.

- Ask for a raise. It'll always be a no if you don't ask, and if you're a valuable employee who contributes more than their fair share, maybe it's time to ask for a little appreciation (in the form of money, not a company lunch).

- Every time your birthday or the holidays roll around, be straight with your family and friends, and tell them you'd rather collect cash instead of pashmina wraps and gift certificates to the mall.

Hot Tips for Fixed Expenses (and Where You Can Save Right Now)

- Be mindful of how much running water you use, and turn the tap off when you can.

- Avoid running your washing machine and dishwasher at peak times; in many cases, those come with surcharges. Stick to evening and weekend laundry.

- Save on electricity and heat by always turning lights off when leaving the room and turning the heat or a/c down when you're leaving the house.

- Call your phone provider about lowering your monthly bill; you'll be surprised how eager they become once you hint at leaving.

- You can also lower your cable bill in the same way and only pay for what you absolutely need. And if the packages are a total scam (99.9 percent of the time, they are), then fuck it. Basic cable and some kind of streaming service like Netflix, Apple TV, or Disney+ is all you need.

- Talk to your bank/credit card provider about lowering your interest rate. (Speaking of lower interest rates, learn how to check your credit score on page 129. If your score improves, you have an excellent case to make for paying less interest. Just sayin'.)

- Top up gas in your car every time you see prices drop.

- Shop smart—in other words, actually open those sale notices and flyers to see what offers are available.

Hot Tips for Variable Expenses (and Being Savvy as Hell)

- Commit to practising essentialism and become aware of how you spend: *Pause and consider.*

- Cut down on restaurant hopping and invite friends over for a home-cooked meal.

- Slow your roll on the takeout and delivery and only use it in emergencies (read: spontaneous visits from friends with three starving kids in tow).

- Book your lady cocktails during happy hour. The discount rate is comical and the people-watching is the best free entertainment around (in financial districts especially).

- Get smart with vacation bookings and avoid peak times (e.g., spring break in South Florida).

- Use travel points wherever applicable and pay attention to point promotions.

- Enter contests for products/experiences you'd like but can't afford (hey, it's worth a shot).

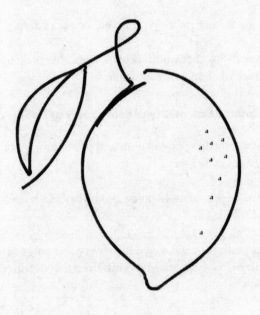

FOOD FOR THOUGHT (LESS WASTE AND MORE MONEY IN YOUR POCKET)

According to recent calculations (2017), the average Canadian household (two adults, two kids) spends about $220 per week on groceries. This, of course, doesn't include eating out, which we know costs a pretty penny in itself. It's suggested to allocate about 15 percent of your household income for food—and once you factor in all household items (like toilet paper, detergent, vitamins, skin care, stupid-expensive diapers) on your list, it adds up fast and can be pretty scary when your income barely covers it.

On top of that, recent findings show that an average Canadian consumer wastes about 375 pounds of food a year, and we're not about that kind of math. Our goal with the tips that follow is to decrease the waste, slash that grocery bill, and help you become the savvy shopper you always imagined yourself to be. (Who knew these would be the things that excite us . . .)

So how much can you actually save? Well, depending on how motivated you are, you stand to save at least 20 percent a year, which could amount to about two thousand bucks. Perhaps enough to cover your next girls' weekend away? Holler!

How to Eat in the '20s (and Beyond)

With notes from Chef Christine Flynn

Much like with fashion, when you buy cheap food (not inexpensive per se, rather low value), someone gets squeezed. It could be the person who grows your food, the person who harvests it, the person who transports it, the person who sells it, or even (if it's not you) the person who cooks it. Reduce how much you spend on groceries just by making smarter decisions that are better for your community and your family, without putting a dent in your wallet.

Get Cooking

We're not asking you to handcuff yourself to the stove. It's 2021, so if you have a partner, talk to them about the best way to divide and conquer meal planning, shopping, and cooking responsibilities. If you're on your own, consider talking to a friend about batch cooking and swapping meals, which will save both of you time, money, and cooking fatigue. You can make several meals for the cost of delivery for two, so if you're committed to cutting down your grocery bill, tie on an apron and make friends with your stove. Cooking can be intimidating if you've never done it before. But hey, you are a mom— you can do anything. Just remember the internet exists, and you can google a video for just about anything you might need to know. Julia Child was almost 40 when she learned to cook; you can do it, too!

Go with the Grain (and the Bean, and the Pulse)

Yes, bread is delicious, but there are all sorts of whole grains, pastas, beans, lentils, and peas that are affordable and easy to cook. Keeping a well-stocked pantry makes it easy to come up with hearty and nutritious meals on the fly, or just to bulk up a soup or stew.

Eat Meatless More Often

Meat is expensive, with good reason. The amount of concern and care it takes to raise an entire animal is huge. If you're looking to reduce your spending, consider going plant-based for the majority of your meals and buying high-quality but less sought-after cuts for a few meals a week.

Learn to Love Leftovers

When you cook, have a plan in place for how you will handle leftovers. Make a quick hash with your leftover mashed potatoes and a half jar of sauerkraut. Turn that leftover flank steak from the weekend into tacos on Tuesday. Chop your grilled veggies from lunch, toss them on a store-bought pizza crust with some shredded cheese, and tell everyone it's a pizza.

Make Ex Ovo Omnia Your Thing

Everything comes from the egg! Cheap, cheerful, *fast*, and a great source of protein, eggs can be prepared a million different ways with little skill.

Buy in Bulk

We'd all like to live next to a farmers' market and wander out each day in search of the perfect baby radishes and maybe some darling little goats' cheese for dinner. If that's your life, God bless. More realistically, you get a few big shops in a month because that's what you have time for, and during the week, you pick up fresh produce and the occasional bunch of herbs. Clear some cupboard space and load up on the essentials (you know, like you did during COVID-19), so you can make a hot meal in the time it takes to say, "What's for dinner, Mama?" Canned tomatoes, beans, and chickpeas (are they beans?), tinned fish (omega-3s, baby), pasta, vegetable or chicken broth, and large-format cheese are all springboards to great meals, and you'll find they are way cheaper when you buy them in volume.

Buy Brand Names on Sale

Always keep your eyes open for those lovely, bright sale tags. Once in a while your favourite brand will be on promo, and that's when you double up and get extra. Coffee is a prime example—that's some shit that you can always stock up on.

Stick to Your Grocery List

Easy right? Kinda. Right up until you're face to face with impulse buys that are begging to jump into your cart (lookin' at you, pre-made seven-layer dip). You can save 23 percent on your bill if you just stick to what you need. This includes being conscious of quantity, too—don't get excited and buy four cucumbers on promo when in fact you'll only use two. This will lessen food waste, which is throwing money into the trash.

Forget Bottled Water

Not only do plastic containers wreak havoc on the environment, but in many cities, the water that comes out of the tap is just as clean as bottled—

sometimes, even cleaner. If you do need the added peace of mind, though, get yourself a Brita filter system and call it a day. And if Perrier is your thing and you like your water sparkly, pick up a SodaStream and you can pump out all the bubbles your heart desires.

Try to Shop Alone

When you can, try to pick up groceries while your kids are locked down at daycare/school/wherever. Shopping with kids can easily add to your grocery bill, with retailers strategically placing tempting items at the eye level of whiny three-year-olds (who will most likely get their way—let's be real).

Pay with Debit/Cash

Studies have shown that people who shop with credit cards almost always spend more than they intended (an average of 10 percent more). It seems pretty obvious why—with cash or debit you can only spend what you have, and it becomes a vastly different grocery trip when you have $100 to your name vs. a $10,000 limit in your pocket.

Talk to Nonna

Sure, sometimes we roll our eyes at our parents' or grandparents' talks of deprivation and having to share shoes with six other siblings at the same time. But hey, they were scrappy enough to get you to this point, and chances are that same nonna who fled Mussolini's Italy with just a canvas bag of zucchini seeds on her back might be able to tell you a thing or two about feeding a lot of people with only a heel of bread and three tomatoes. Ask around—everyone has a "struggle meal" they keep in their back pocket, and while it won't always be delicious, it might be, and it usually comes with a great story.

Have a Garden Party

Getting down and dirty takes on a whole new meaning for a mother, but we really encourage you to stick a couple pots on your tiny deck or windowsill, and poke some seeds in there. You don't need a ton of space to grow herbs, tomatoes, peppers, or (if you fancy) edible flowers and lettuces. Plus, it gives you something to look after that doesn't talk back.

Invest in Organic

In Canada, organic isn't just about the quality of the food you are buying. Organic means that the land the food is grown on is also carefully maintained, and that the people growing and harvesting the food are treated fairly. For many farmers, switching to organic was initially too expensive to be a reasonable business model. But now that more people are purchasing organic, more farmers are able to transition to that model, and many of them are even able to purchase larger amounts of seed at a lower price because they are buying in bulk. If you are financially able, consider putting your dollars into organic. It tastes better, it's better for our planet, and while it's not a perfect system, when you invest in organic as a model, you're making it more accessible for everyone.

Oh, and one last piece of advice: Don't pull a rookie move and shop on an empty stomach.

You know how that ends.

A Chef-Worthy Recipe to Get You Started

By Christine Flynn

Pescado Pasta

Look, I gave this an Italian name because it sounds fancy and like something that might take you all afternoon to make. It's not; but no one has to know except us. This is one of those recipes you can knock together in about 10 minutes (or as long as it takes to cook the pasta), and you really don't need to go out of your way to buy anything fancy. Tinned fish gets a bad rap on the North American continent, but it's actually one of the most sustainable protein options (look for the MSC or Marine Stewardship Council logo), and it comes packed in flavourful olive oil, which often just gets poured down the sink even though it has a million different uses. A little tinned fish, some pasta, a squeeze of lemon, fresh herbs from your window pot, and stale bread turn into more than the sum of their parts with this recipe. Feel free to add things like chopped tomatoes, olives, chili flakes, or whatever is slowly turning soft in the back of your crisper. Serve with chilled Chablis, or, you know, with whatever white blend comes in the big box you keep wedged under the condiments shelf in your fridge.

Serves 4–6

    1 lb (450 g) dried spaghetti or fettuccine
    2–3 stale slices of white or whole-wheat bread
    2 Tbsp (30 mL) olive oil, divided
    2 x 4-ounce (106 g) tins of sardines packed in olive oil
    3 cloves of garlic, smashed
    Zest and juice of 2 lemons
    Splash of white wine (optional)
    Small handful of capers, roughly chopped (optional)
    Salt and pepper to taste
    Large handful of flat leaf or Italian parsley, roughly chopped
    1/2 cup (125 mL) finely grated Grana Padano or Asiago cheese

In a large pot, bring 16 cups (4 L) of salted water to a boil. Cook pasta for 2 minutes less than the package instructs. Reserve about 1 cup (250 mL) of the pasta water. Drain, but do not rinse, the pasta (you want it to stay starchy) and set aside on a large baking sheet while you prepare the rest of the ingredients. Wipe out the pot, but do not wash.

Place the stale bread in a food processor or blender, and pulse briefly to make bread crumbs. In the large pot you used to cook the spaghetti, heat 1 Tbsp (15 mL) olive oil over medium-high heat until it just shimmers. Add the bread crumbs and turn down heat to medium. Toast the bread crumbs until golden brown, and then set aside on a plate. Wipe out the pot, but do not wash.

In the same large pot over medium heat, drain the oil from the sardines, and add remaining olive oil and smashed garlic. Heat the garlic in the sardine oil gently until it is golden brown, about 4–5 minutes. Once the garlic is brown, break it down with the back of a wooden spoon, or simply pull it out and discard. Add in the fish and stir briefly. Don't worry if it falls apart a bit; this is a rustic dish. If you happen to have a splash of white wine—either for you or for the pasta—now would be a great time for it. Add the reserved pasta water and the zest and juice of both lemons, as well as capers, if using, to the sardine mixture. Add the pasta back into the pot, and continue to cook for 2 minutes, until the pasta is cooked through and hot. Check seasoning, and add salt and pepper to taste. Turn off heat. Top with parsley, bread crumbs, and cheese. Serve immediately and refrigerate leftovers for up to 5 days.

COMPOUND INTEREST (YOUR BFF)

Compound interest means that the interest you earn on your savings also earns interest and the interest on that interest earns interest, ad infinitum. Basically, it's a method of increasing your savings without having to do shit.

The biggest benefit of compound interest is that you make a lot more money than you do with simple interest. In fact, there's something called the Law of 72 that says that the number 72 divided by the annual interest rate is the number of years it will take to double your money without ever contributing a cent.

That means if your interest rate is 5 percent, it would take you something like 14 years to double your money.

BOOM. That's the kind of math we like.

Here's a basic example of how compound interest compares to simple interest:

Let's say you have $100 in the bank and your interest rate is 5 percent per year.

First, simple interest:

Year 1: $100 + $5 = $105 ($5 in interest)

Year 2: $105 + $5 = $110 ($5 in interest)

Year 3: $110 + $5 = $115 ($5 in interest)

Now compare that to compound interest, wherein the interest you earn also earns interest:

Year 1: $100 + 5 percent = $105 ($5 in interest)

Year 2: $105 + 5 percent = $110.25 ($5.25 in interest)

Year 3: $110.25 + 5 percent = $115.76 ($5.51 in interest)

It may not seem like much, but it sure adds up over time (especially if you're continuously adding to the pot). Think of it as a tiny ball of snow you set rolling down a hill. The longer the hill, the bigger the snowball will be when it reaches the bottom.

The other factor is how often the interest is compounded or added to your balance. The more frequently the money is compounded (some types of accounts compound monthly or even daily!), the faster it grows.

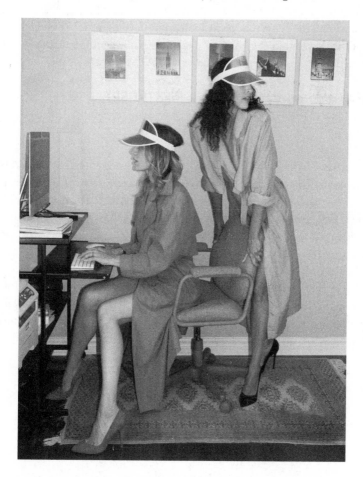

TAX SHELTERING 101

Tax sheltering means putting certain amounts of money into specific savings accounts that help you avoid paying tax on a portion of your earnings, thereby keeping your money where you want it: in your pocketbook.

This is not something you want to write off as just one of those things rich people do. That's not to say that it *isn't* one of those things rich people do—it definitely is. But it's important to remove any of the phrase's negative connotations from your brain immediately because tax sheltering is fair, legal, and important AF for you to participate in in the long run. Let's take a closer look at the three main categories of tax-sheltered accounts in Canada so that you can decide which ones are right for you ATM.

Registered Retirement Savings Plan (RRSP)

What Is It?

A Registered Retirement Savings Plan (RRSP) is an account introduced by the Canadian government in 1957 to help Canadians save for retirement. It has since expanded its programs to include an **RRSP Home Buyers' Plan (HBP)** and an **RRSP Lifelong Learning Plan (LLP)**, which were designed to help Canadians save for a first-home down payment and continued education respectively. RRSPs are "tax-deferred," meaning any money you contribute will be exempt from CRA taxes the year you make the deposit, and will only be taxed years down the line when you withdraw it. The main benefit of RRSPs is that tax on RRSP contributions is deferred until retirement (a time of life when you're subject to much lower tax rates). In short, RRSPs are an amazing way to cut down a current-year tax bill.

Who Can/Should Open One?

There are two types of people for whom an RRSP is ideal:

1. Those who are saving specifically to buy a house

2. Those who make more than $50,000 per year and are focused on saving specifically for retirement

Note: If you make *less* than $50,000 per year and are focused on retirement, you'll want to look into a TFSA (see page 176).

The only conditions for eligibility are that you are under 71 years of age, are a Canadian resident for tax purposes, and file income taxes in Canada. Minors under the age of 18 can set up an RRSP with written parental consent (or that of a legal guardian).

How Do You Open One?

Opening an RRSP requires very little time and energy and can easily be accomplished from the comfort of your own home. You've got tons of choices of institutions wherein you might open an RRSP account (every bank ever plus some online options that will likely incur less fees). Before you take the plunge, do a little research and find out which is best for you and your family's current needs (more on page 188).

How Do Deposits Work?

Because RRSPs are registered accounts, they're subject to certain rules. One of the most important rules concerns the amount of money you can contribute to the account in any given year; it's either 18 percent of your past year's income or a maximum amount, whichever's smaller. (For reference, in 2019 the RRSP deduction limit was $26,500. In 2020 the limit was $27,230—the amount may increase annually.)

You can also catch up if you didn't max out your investments in earlier years; to find out how much you can contribute, check out the Notice of Assessment you got after filing your taxes last year.

It's important to remember that even though you might have contribution room left over from previous years, you will *not* accumulate deduction limits. Let's say you made $100,000 last year and you have some RRSP contribution room remaining from previous years, so you decide to deposit

$36,000 into your account. This contribution would be accepted, but you would be able to deduct only $18,000 (18 percent of your income) from your current-year taxes.

How Do Withdrawals Work?

Depending on the kind of RRSP owner you are (retiree or homebuyer), withdrawals will work in one of two ways:

1. **For an RRSP withdrawal by a retiree:** When you retire, your RRSP turns into a Registered Retirement Income Fund (RRIF) that you can withdraw money from (income tax would apply to any withdrawals). When you die, however, your RRSP is usually rolled over to a beneficiary on a tax-deferred basis. (Remember that will we told you to make a while back? If you open an RRSP—or any tax sheltering account, for that matter—you'll want to add a note on who you'd like to be the beneficiary for that account in case you croak; if no beneficiary has been named, then the proceeds from your RRSP are considered part of your estate and will be distributed accordingly).

2. **For an RRSP withdrawal by a homebuyer:** The RRSP Home Buyers' Plan allows eligible first-time homebuyers to withdraw up to $35,000 tax-free from their RRSP to be used toward a down payment on the purchase of the home. To withdraw funds, first you'll need to fill out form T1036. This is called the "Home Buyers' Plan (HBP) Request to Withdraw Funds from a RRSP." You should submit this form to your financial institution to let them know your intention to withdraw funds. It's not possible to withdraw the money from your RRSP and then claim it was part of the Home Buyers' Plan, so make sure to do it the right way! Note that it's very possible to make multiple withdrawals under the Home Buyers' Plan in the same year, provided you don't exceed the $35,000 limit.

It's important to note that the Home Buyer's Plan is structured in such a way that you're basically loaning yourself money for a house, and because of that, it comes with a hell of a lot of rules—rules with great tax implications that you'll definitely need to follow. If you're planning to purchase your first home sooner rather than later, you may want to consider a more accessible account. A TFSA might be the wiser choice since they're a lot more lenient about withdrawals than RRSPs.

Whether you're using the funds in this account for retirement or to help you with a down payment on your first home, you may be wondering just how much you will have made on your investment when it's time to withdraw. What you should know is that the value of your RRSP depends on how much you've contributed each year, what assets your RRSP is invested in, and how many years you've had the account for. However, average rates of return for retirement accounts tend to hover between 4 and 8 percent.

But what if you *really* need to access funds from your RRSP before retirement? Well, it's possible, but if you withdraw from your RRSP before you turn 71, that withdrawal will count as income—meaning you'll be taxed on the amount at a higher tax rate than you probably would if you withdrew it during retirement. You will also be charged a withholding tax, and you'll permanently lose the contribution room you used to originally make your deposit.

Alright, let's pause here for a moment to stare at this magnificent photo and remind ourselves of all the wonderful things and experiences our savings can buy.

After Contributing to My RRSP, What Comes Next?

That would be the good old TFSA . . .

Tax-Free Savings Account (TFSA)

What Is It?

A Tax-Free Savings Account (TFSA) is a registered investment or savings account that allows for tax-free gains. The amount of money that can be contributed to a TFSA is limited each year. A TFSA can be used for any savings goal, and withdrawals can be made free of tax.

Who Can/Should Open One?

Any Canadian who is 18 years of age or older with a valid social insurance number (SIN) can open a TFSA. TFSAs are usually preferable for both lower earners and those who think they may need to access their funds before retirement. If the funds you're investing are for your retirement, TFSAs are generally considered preferable to RRSPs for those earning less than $50,000 a year.

How Do You Open One?

All you need to do is reach out to a financial institution, credit union, or online investment company that offers TFSAs and provide your SIN and date of birth. It's likely they'll ask you for supporting documents like a birth certificate to prove you are who you say you are. Unless you're trying to impersonate someone else, the process shouldn't take more than 10 minutes to complete.

How Do Deposits Work?

The government-mandated maximum you're allowed to put into a TFSA each year is known as the contribution limit and it varies from year to year. In 2019, for example, it was $6,000. It's a good idea to take a gander at this year's limit and past limits before you open a TFSA and start contributing.

That's because over-contributing comes with a nasty little penalty—1 percent of the excess contribution every month until it's withdrawn.

How Do Withdrawals Work?

Unlike an RRSP, you're free to withdraw from your TFSA account at any time without penalty. When you do withdraw money from a TFSA, the amount you take out is added to how much you can contribute the following year. And TFSA contribution room doesn't disappear if you fail to contribute in any given year. It just rolls over into the next year so you'll have an ever-expanding contribution limit.

After Contributing to a TFSA and an RRSP, What Comes Next?

First off, good for you! If you've been a busy saver, have stocked up your emergency fund, and are contributing to an RRSP and a TFSA, it's time to start diversifying your investments further, if you haven't done so already. A personal investment account, for example, can help you explore other investment opportunities once your retirement savings are in a good place . . . But for those of us who have children, a Registered Education Savings Plan (RESP) is probably a better move.

Registered Education Savings Plan (RESP)

What Is It?

RESPs are tax-advantaged accounts (read: tax-deferral/tax-exception vessels) designed to help Canadians save for higher education. RESP funds can be invested in countless ways, and if they are spent on higher-education related tuition or expenses, no investment gains in the account will be subject to income taxes. Arguably the most epic thing about RESPs is the access they provide to the Canada Education Savings Grant (CESG)—a program that promises to match 20 percent of any RESP contributions up to $2,500 per account, per child, per year. (Note to non-math majors: That means the government would kick in a maximum $500 per kid.) Kids from lower-income households are eligible for even more CESG money.

RESPs can be opened by any adult with a SIN, on behalf of any child with a SIN. They are non-transferable except to a sibling. A **family RESP**, however, can be opened only by parents or grandparents and may be spent on the education of any child in the family.

Who Can/Should Open One?

As long as both the account opener and beneficiary are Canadian, it doesn't matter who opens the account. It could be a child's parent, a grandparent, a friend of the family, or any old benevolent neighbour with a nice pile of cash and a soft spot for your kid.

How Do You Open One?

All you'll need are two social insurance numbers (SINs), your own and the beneficiary's, and a vetted financial institution whose rates, fees, and service you feel comfortable with. You can open one in person (at a bank, for example) or through an online investor.

How Do Deposits Work?

Under current law you can contribute a lifetime maximum of $50,000 per beneficiary to an RESP. The amount of annual contribution room that is eligible for the CESG is $2,500. You are welcome to contribute more, but the 20 percent grant is only matched by the government up to $2,500 per year. Your contribution room is accrued each year starting in 2007 or the year the child was born, whichever is later. The contribution room keeps accruing up to and including the year the child turns 17, so it's possible to harness that free CESG government money even if you miss out on a year or two.

To maximize the CESG, you will want to contribute $2,500 per year per beneficiary for 14 years, and then top it off with an extra $1,000 in the 15th year. This is because the total amount of CESG money a child can receive is $7,200. If you missed a year or started late, you can contribute more than $2,500 to retroactively claim grants. You are eligible to receive an additional $500 per year in CESG if you missed previous years' grants. In short, you can catch up for one previous year at a time by contributing more than $2,500 per year.

How Do Withdrawals Work?

There a number of rules that come with owning an RESP, many of which are specific to the withdrawal of RESP money. Here are the basics of what you should know before you attempt to take money out of your RESP:

- Only the person who set up the account and made contributions can make withdrawals—they're known as the subscriber. Withdrawals of contributions made by the subscriber are called Post-Secondary Education (PSE) withdrawals. They may be sent to either the subscriber or beneficiary. Withdrawals of the government grant/bond portion (known as the Education Assistance Payments or EAPs) can only be sent to the beneficiary.

- The subscriber must provide the financial institution that holds the RESP with a student's proof of enrollment before being able to access funds.

- PSE withdrawals aren't taxable. The student will be taxed on EAPs, which consist of both investment gains as well as government grant money. The financial company that holds the RESP will issue a T4A tax form in the student's name for EAPs only.

- There is a $5,000 limit on withdrawals of EAP contributions during the first 13 weeks of full-time schooling (or $2,500 if the student is enrolled part-time), effectively eliminating the possibility that one first-year student will be forced to purchase beer for an entire university. There is no limit on the amount of subscriber PSE contributions that can be withdrawn. Once the 13 weeks have passed, any amount of EAP contributions can be withdrawn.

After Contributing to My RESP, What Comes Next?

Celebrations. All of the celebrations.

Part 6

INVESTING

Investing is the final frontier in the quest for financial freedom. It's what turns savings into wealth and allows you to retire one day *stress-fucking-free*.

INVESTING 101

If you've got money in an RRSP or a TFSA, then you're already in the game. These accounts are vessels in which you can really begin to put your money to work. Perhaps you're thinking, *But those accounts are so long-term!* Yes, they are, and that's the point. Unless you are rich AF and can stand to lose a shit-ton of money in the not-so-distant future, then pretty much all of your investments *should* be long-term and your risk tolerance should be low.

If your goals are more short-term—meaning you'll need to use returns within the next few years—a savings or money market account that offers interest with virtually no risk of a fall in value might be the best choice.

However, if you're ready to commit for the long haul, then listen up. Investing is not a sprint or a 100-metre dash; it's a marathon. And training begins now.

Assets and Liabilities

If we have learned anything through the process of researching and writing this book, it's this: *With each dollar that enters your hand, you have the power to determine your destiny.* You will attain financial freedom if you use your money to invest in your mind—read books, solicit advice from the right people—*and learn how to acquire assets.*

To clarify: An **asset** is anything you own that puts money *in* your pocket. A **liability**, on the other hand, is anything you own that takes money *out* of your pocket. Your mortgage? Consumer loans? Credit cards? Antique teacup collection? Car? All liabilities. Stocks? Bonds? Notes? Real estate? Intellectual property? Those are the assets. Those are the money-makers.

To paraphrase Robert Kiyosaki, author of *Rich Dad Poor Dad*, if you want financial freedom, spend your life buying assets. If you don't, spend your life buying liabilities. It really is that simple.

So how do you start acquiring assets? Where do you even begin?

First, you'll need a basic understanding of your options—what are the different kinds of things you can invest your money in? Then, you'll want to assess your time horizon (what are your goals and how long-term are they?) and your risk tolerance. The last step is to take those learnings and apply them to finding yourself the best possible source for upfront advice based on your individual circumstances. In other words: Get ye a fucking solid financial advisor or trusted online robo-advisor. Unless you're prepared to dedicate years to learning the financial system inside out, your responsibility is to learn just enough to help you discern who to trust with your hard-earned dough.

Investment Options

Assets come in many forms. Some are tangible (like real estate and gold bars), but most are intangible. We called in the experts at Wealthsimple one last time to help us break down a few examples of vehicles that can be used to invest money from an RRSP, a TFSA, or an RESP.

Guaranteed Investment Certificates (GICs)

A GIC is a financial product that allows you to lend money to a bank at a fixed interest rate for a predetermined amount of time (usually between three months and five years)—the longer the term, the better the interest gains will be. It's one of the lowest-risk investments out there, making it an easy way to maintain, if not accumulate, funds. If you're looking to diversify your investments (note: You should always be looking for ways to diversity investments!), you may be well served to use GICs to balance an otherwise high-risk portfolio so you know that at least a portion of your stash is safe.

Bonds

A bond is a loan agreement between a borrower (the bond issuer) and a lender (the bondholder). The former needs money and is willing to pay interest to get it; the latter has money to lend but needs to be compensated with interest to lend it. Voila! A match made in finance heaven. Interest on the loan is paid monthly throughout the life of the bond. Once the bond has matured, the borrower pays back the lender's initial investment, and everyone moves on with their lives.

Bonds and GICs are both boring AF and safe AF. They earn predetermined payouts, so they won't fall in value, plus bondholders get paid before shareholders if a company goes bankrupt.

There are eight different types of bonds: sovereign government bonds, municipal bonds, agency bonds, investment-grade corporate bonds, convertible bonds, foreign bonds, non-conventional bonds, and junk bonds. Out of these, only junk bonds (also known as "high-yield" or "speculative" bonds) are considered high risk.

Stocks

Public corporations can allow people to buy a portion of company shares (note: shares = units of stock) in an effort to raise funds to grow and operate their business. The person who buys the stock becomes a part owner of the company (a.k.a. a shareholder).

According to Kimberly Amadeo, US economy expert for The Balance, there are two ways to make money off stocks. The first is by selling shares for more than the purchasing price. The second is through dividends, which are paid to shareholders (usually quarterly) out of company earnings.

Amadeo notes that there are two main types of shares you can buy in a company: common and preferred. Common shareholders have voting rights that can be exercised in corporate decisions, whereas preferred shareholders do not. Both types of shares are conducive to dividend earnings; however, preferred shareholders are paid an agreed-upon dividend at regular intervals (making preferred shares similar, in theory, to bonds), whereas common shareholders' dividend payouts depend entirely on how much money the corporation made in any given quarter. Stocks definitely carry with them more risk than bonds and GICs do (especially common shares), but they also offer the possibility of greater rewards.

Mutual Funds

While not all mutual funds are RRSP-eligible, most are, and they're a great way for investors to purchase multiple stocks, bonds, and other assets at one time. These bundles are assembled, priced, and actively traded once a day by fund managers. Since mutual funds often contain hundreds of stocks and bonds, investing in them will automatically diversify your investment, giving you some natural protection from market volatility.

There are three ways you can make money off mutual funds:

1. **Dividend payments:** Income is earned from dividends on stocks and interest on bonds held in the fund's portfolio. A fund pays out nearly all of the income it receives over the year to fund owners in the form of an annual distribution. Funds often give investors a choice to either receive a cheque for distributions or reinvest the earnings and get more shares.

2. **Capital gains:** When a fund sells a security that has gone up in price, this is a capital gain. When a fund sells a security that has gone down in price, this is a capital loss. Most funds distribute any net capital gains to investors annually.

3. **Net asset value (NAV):** If fund holdings increase in price but aren't sold by the fund manager, the fund's shares increase in price. This is similar to when the price of a stock increases—you don't receive immediate distributions, but the value of your investment is greater, and you will make money if you decide to sell.

Exchange-Traded Funds (ETF)

An ETF is a collection of stocks or bonds that may be purchased for one price. They're called "exchange-traded" funds because they can be bought and sold during the entire trading day, just like individual stocks (and unlike mutual funds). Consider the ETF to be a relative of the mutual fund; the two are similar but not the same. The main difference? Mutual funds are actively managed (by a person) and ETFs are passively managed (by a computer). Because most ETFs don't require humans to make trading decisions, they tend to come with lower fees (keep in mind that fees tend to add up in a big way over time—especially when it comes to investments).

There is a shit-ton of different kinds of ETFs you can buy. There are some designed to mirror the entire stock market (they're called stock market tracking ETFs, and they're the most popular ones) and others that encapsulate stocks from an entire sector.

Purchasing an ETF containing dozens, if not hundreds, of stocks, will automatically diversify your investment over the purchase of one stock, and you will be afforded some natural protection for your investment from market volatility.

Remember, if you're like most people (i.e., you're not fuck-you rich), you're going to want to use your investment account to create a highly diverse portfolio including a little bit of each type of investment. The most cost-effective way to do that is to buy a whole index, such as the TSX (Canada), the DOW/Nasdaq/S&P (US), and various others worldwide, using vessels like mutual funds and ETFs. Buying individual stocks—as romanticized as it often is—should be left to the professionals.

But no matter what you want to invest in, the process will have to begin with you opening an investment account, and the sooner you do that, the sooner you'll take advantage of compound interest and grow your nest egg.

START INVESTING EARLY

to save $1 million by age 65, you'd have to invest 28K every year starting at age 45. if you start at 25, you'd only have to invest 7k/year.

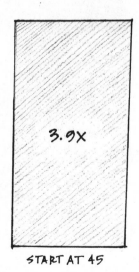

3.9X

1X

START AT 25   START AT 45

FINDING A SOLID ADVISOR

Now, let's talk about those professionals. There are a few different people/ institutions that will try to convince you to trust them with your money, namely: bricks-and-mortar banks, financial advisors/firms, discount brokerages, and automated investment services. This is a big decision to make, considering your financial future is at stake (no pressure), so you'll want to do your research. Start with this table:

	Pros	Cons
Resident Advisor at a Bricks-and-Mortar Bank	• Convenience (you're already pretty much set up there) • Familiarity • Free coffee	• They're likely not legally bound to make decisions based on your best interest (only someone with the title of "fiduciary" is). • They're likely to advise based on meeting sales quotas for "affiliated funds" (created by the bank itself). Not only might these be the wrong investments for your needs, but they may also be laced with fees.
Financial Advisor (Individual or Firm)	• Convenience (it's part of their job to be available to you) • Human connection with someone who (hopefully) knows what the hell they're doing	• You'll have to commit a certain amount of time and energy to finding the ideal candidate. • They're likely to charge high fees that can really add up when compounded with fees already built into investment tools like mutual funds and ETFs. • The probability of human error

	Pros	Cons
Discount Brokerage	• Inexpensive • Gives you direct access to the assets you're looking to buy	• Not recommended for anyone who is not an expert or close to it (Malcolm Gladwell has defined an expert as someone who has spent 10,000 hours studying any one subject or practising any one skill—use this to evaluate your own level of expertise) • Errors made here are very, very expensive (rule of thumb: If you do try a discount brokerage, make sure you're only playing with an amount of money you're comfortable losing. That should be less than 1 percent of your overall savings)
Automated Service	• Convenience (usually they come in the form of an app or a user-friendly website) • Low fees • Robots are great at math	• Possibly intimidating for the technologically challenged (although the good ones are simple enough that set-up should only take five minutes, no matter how tech-savvy you are) • No face-to-face interaction (not much of a con these days, though) • Could be a total scam (word to the wise: If you call the number listed on the site and are unable to speak with a human representative . . . run)

Remember, the goal here is not to be the Wolf of Wall Street by the time you're done reading this book. People study and work for years to figure out how this shit actually works. Just as you trust your doctor with your medical needs and your accountant with your accounting needs, you need to find people in the financial space to address your financial needs. Your goal should be to ensure that you understand *enough* that you won't get ripped off, be sold a shitty plan, or get expertly fucked over by a shady account manager or advisory firm.

Things to Sort Out Before Looking for an Advisor

1. **Your investment goals:** Some typical goals might include

   - saving for your retirement;

   - saving for your children's education;

   - buying a house; or

   - starting a business.

It is not uncommon to be investing for multiple goals simultaneously. Knowing your goals will help you figure out your time horizon.

2. **Your time horizon:** A longer time horizon allows you to take more investment risk since you have ample time to make up losses from the market corrections that will inevitably occur over time.

A longer time horizon also allows investors to take advantage of perhaps the biggest single tool available: compounding (you may remember the concept from page 170). That's why everyone in the financial world will tell you that the best time to start saving and investing is *now*. This allows you to take advantage of the "magic" of compounding gains over time.

3. **Your risk tolerance:** Risk tolerance is your ability to weather losses in your portfolio. While nobody likes to lose money, investors should consider that the stock market ebbs and flows, and it *will* decline from time to time. Your modus operandi should be to work with an advisor (be it robo or human) to figure out a long-term plan that you can decide on and stick to—through good times and bad—until retirement.

Your risk tolerance should be aligned with the time horizon of the goals you are trying to achieve. A longer-term goal like saving for retirement allows you to take a bit more risk since you have time to recover from losses. A shorter-term goal like buying a house in the next couple of years does not allow for a lot of risk, and your investments tied to this goal should reflect this.

Speaking of retirement goals . . .

INVESTING: LEVEL EXPERT

Now, what if you're absolutely killing it? You've got cash at your fingertips in your chequing account and an emergency cushion in your savings account; you've got your TFSA, RRSP, and RESP contributions maxed; and now you're looking for ways to manage all your excess cash.

First, fucking bravo. That is not an easy feat and you should take a moment to pat yourself on the back for being so GD fiscally responsible. Feel free to go pour yourself a cocktail and propose a toast to your awesomeness. We'll wait.

1 PT. GIN
1 PT. CAMPARI
1 PT. SWT. VERMOUTH

+ cube of ice
+ orange rind

Oh, good—you're back. Where were we? Ah, yes, you were taking inventory of all your surplus cash and wondering what to do with it all.

Depending on how close you are to retirement, once you've maxed out your tax-safe investment accounts, there's a good chance you'll be able to afford to take greater risk (and potentially make greater gains). Yes, those earnings will be taxed at a high rate, but who cares? You're rich, yo!

In this case, you'll be looking for some other ways to invest that'll help you diversify further.

Your options here include

- buying real estate;

- picking stocks (only 5 percent of your portfolio should be dedicated to single stocks, though);

- becoming an angel investor; and

- purchasing select collectibles (cars, watches, art, etc.).

The best way to decide what to do with a massive cash surplus (again, congrats and please invite us on your yacht) is to let your passions lead you to exciting investment opportunities. Do you have a hobby that could turn into a lucrative investment possibility? Have you always had an interest in something you never pursued and want to try your hand at it? Well, now is the time, sis. The work is over—now it's time to play! Just remember, if you reach this point and you're not having fun, then you're not doing it right.

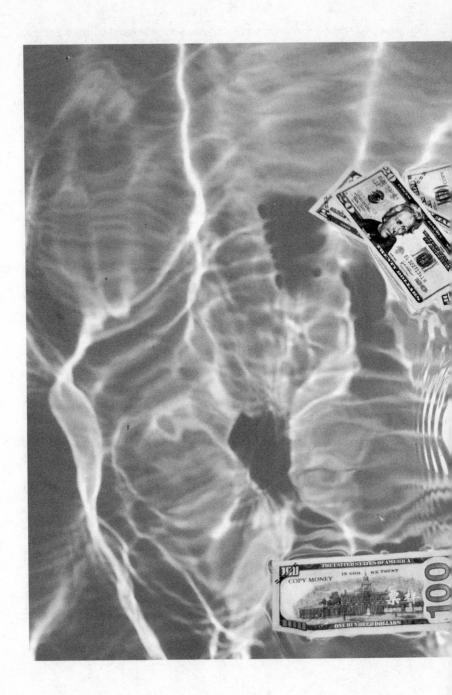

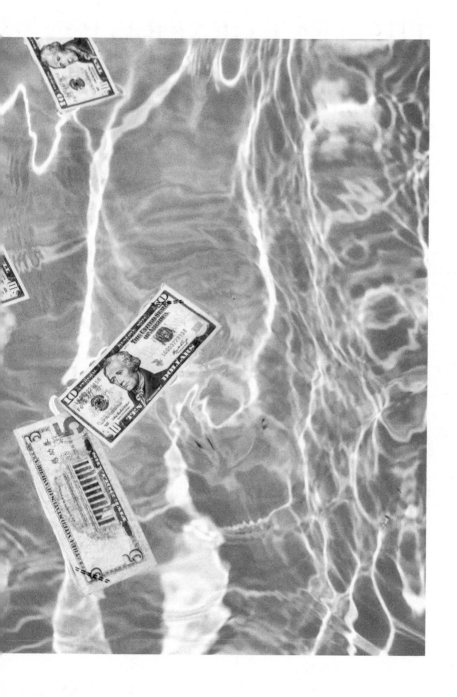

THE NEXT GENERATION (THE BIGGEST INVESTMENT OF ALL)

Hopefully by now you're feeling more comfortable with financial concepts and terms, but even if you don't fancy yourself a money whiz just yet, you should still aim to get your offspring involved and start imparting some financial wisdom early on.

But I've been fiscally irresponsible my whole life! What kind of example will I be for my kids?

Oh, babe, don't worry about it. It's perfectly fine if you have made money mistakes in the past—we all have. It certainly doesn't mean you're a bad example in the present. The important thing is to develop your own financial goals, commit to working toward them now, and talk openly about money at home. Just don't make it a tip-toe topic for everyone to awkwardly avoid.

So, what do the kids need to know? Let's start with the basics:

- We work to earn money—explain what that work looks like for your family.

- Money allows us to have things we need and want.

- Everything from electricity and tap water to their dance class and lightsaber fetish costs money.

- Some things cost less; some things, more—discuss pricing and buying decisions when shopping.

- We are sold to all day—point out ads as you see them and identify what they're selling.

Once you start weaving these conversations into your daily life as a family, your kids will quickly start grasping the idea of money, which may help prevent them from becoming entitled dicks down the road. (Fingers crossed, anyway.)

Of course, the next question you may have is *When should I start teaching the young about money?*

Although it's never too early to teach kids to respect the value of a dollar, it's probably most sensible to wait until they can somewhat grasp the bigger concepts you're putting forward—which is usually around the time they enter kindergarten (at age four or five) or when they become naturally curious about it themselves.

But how exactly do I go about teaching my kids about money?

We've compiled some tips and conversation starters for you.

Earning

You don't want to teach your child that money falls from the sky (even if it flows freely out of Nonna's purse). You will want to instill a system early on that will have your kid performing tasks or completing chores in exchange for money (ideas include laundry, recycling, shovelling snow). Be reasonable with the rates vs. quality expectations of said tasks, and treat the whole process seriously by organizing an envelope for pay. A good rule of thumb is paying their age per week with a payout at the end of the month.

Saving

You want to get your kid into saving early on so it's not a huge slap in the face when they exit university and life has its way with them. (Hello, have you seen rent prices lately?) Save 30 percent of earnings—so if they have racked up their monthly pay of a whopping $20, then $6 of that will automatically go into the savings envelope.

Giving

Kindness and empathy can't begin soon enough, and although donating toys and clothes to those less fortunate is a great starting point, putting their actual money (say, 10 percent) toward a good cause is something that will not only make them feel good, but will also build on those morals for the future. Hand over some decision-making power by allowing your child to choose where that money goes—whether the charity supports the homeless, animals, children, or another good cause, it's a good conversation to have.

Spending

Ah, the fun part! Well, if 30 percent has gone to saving and another 10 percent to giving, that leaves your mini tycoon with 60 percent of $20, which is $12 and just enough to buy that action hero they've been coveting and maybe a bag of Skittles. Here you may also have the opportunity to explain to your child what their disposable income really means—i.e., "Mama will get the necessities such as food, water, and literally everything else under this roof and beyond, and you get to spend your money on some fun stuff for you." Try not to mutter "must be nice" right after.

What if my child doesn't do all the chores?

Then they don't get their allowance. Period. This is the most important value you will teach them, because in the real world, you cannot perform a portion of your job and still get paid.

What if my kid becomes so obsessed with saving, they don't want to spend at all?

Kids can definitely swing to extremes, and although saving all their cash seems like a genius idea, you want them to have a healthy balance and be able to enjoy the fruits of their labour. If they're trying to save for something big, you can even offer to match contributions to see their efforts through.

Oh, One More Thing: Kid Branding

It's so common that you may have missed it as it flew by right under your nose (read: Barbie's American Express card). Corporations know well that this early seeding will influence your tiny, naïve human later in life, and they are all vying to be subconsciously top of mind when the time is right. With kids being targeted so early, it's our moral responsibility as parents to make sure we get there first. Besides, literally no one wants a spoiled brat running around with their credit card, and this is one way to curb that whole debacle.

Take your kid with you to the bank and open an account for them. Involve them in the process, with you by their side. This will empower them and give them a sense of accountability. Any self-proclaimed "big kid" will squirm with excitement at feeling like an adult for a day, and the bank sure knows how to make them feel special—in many cases, adding to your opening contributions with their own (legitimately the only time in their lives they will ever receive free money from the bank).

At the end of the day, we want to raise our kids to be financially responsible adults, and the sooner we stop treating money like a dirty little secret that is "impolite" to discuss, the better off we (as a whole society) will be.

And remember, have fun! This whole process does not have to be daunting/boring/equivalent to a root canal gone bad. Keep it light, ask if the kids understand something, and explain (transparently) if they don't. Eventually, money will become a normalized topic, which will most certainly benefit your kids from their upbringing through to adulthood.

IN CLOSING

So how are we feeling? Enlightened? Empowered? Emboldened? Ready to start smoking cigars and shooting the shit about investment portfolios on the golf course?

Yeah, baby, that's the spirit!

Note: From a strategic standpoint, learning to golf may not be the worst idea . . . So many business deals are made and so much financial advice is doled out while driving around on those stupid carts that it would make your fucking head spin.

But before you get drunk on vodka-spiked Arnold Palmers and start looking for second-hand golf clubs on the internet (how all great golfers begin their foray into the sport), let's take advantage of these last moments together and make some commitments to one another about the type of relationship we plan to forge with our finances going forward.

Let's agree to approach money with the right attitude; we know that when it comes to the game of finance, mindset plays a vital role. Let's vow to show ourselves the respect we deserve. Repeat the following aloud:

I am capable; I am informed; I am ready to use finance as a means of empowerment.

From this day forth, I will view money as something to put to work for me, rather than something to work for.

There is no time like the present to make this commitment to yourself (compound interest alone should be reason enough). Make a conscious decision to spend your life buying assets and building wealth. Invest in yourself—in your knowledge and skill set. Be calculated and be strategic. Plan. Budget. Work hard. Free yourself from debt, spend consciously, and think carefully about what kind of earner you'll be once you procreate. Whether you're a Bo$$, Hu$tler, $cholar, or $AHM, know that there will be obstacles galore on the road to your financial freedom. That's okay. Embrace them, knowing that enduring hard shit only makes you stronger and more resilient in the long run.

Now that you have a foundation of financial literacy to build upon, let your curiosity run wild. Read books! Ask questions! Seek sound advice! Carpe that motherfucking diem! Talk about money management with the most successful people you know. Have frank conversations about your goals with your partner and strategize together on how to achieve them. This is the highest form of self-care out there, babe—don't let billboards and blog posts convince you otherwise.

And remember, none of this constitutes some pie-in-the-sky pipe dream. Financial freedom is absolutely within your reach, no matter how many small, revenue-negative roommates you've got living under your roof. The system (well, the Canadian system, anyway) was literally designed to help you get there. Take advantage of that. Understand that this is society's way of investing in you and your endless potential.

Our Queen (Oprah) once said that what you ask for from the world is exactly what you are getting back. Our advice? Ask big. Refuse to reduce your goals.

Know your worth.
(Now double it).

ACKNOWLEDGEMENTS

We would like to first acknowledge the women who picked up this book, learned from it, did the work, and recommended it to their sisters, friends, and fellow moms. Financial understanding puts you in the power position, ladies, and that's exactly where you belong.

To our partners, Anthony and Jeff—thank you for recognizing the importance of this project and responding by being supportive AF, providing us with the time and space to get shit done, and stepping into the primary caregiver role more than ever. We promise not to invest behind your back.

To the year 2020—kudos to you for making us *even more* efficient than before by pairing the tightest book deadline ever with a climate disaster, global pandemic, and civil rights uprising. Luckily, we still got it done despite the kids crawling on our heads. We've honestly never felt more badass.

To our kids—you are the best investment we've ever made. It's all for you guys.

To Wealthsimple—we literally couldn't have written this book without you. Thank you for being the financial resource of our dreams and helping us bring this vision to life.

To Arthur Stanley—thank you for blessing us with your infinite knowledge of all things finance and business. You are living proof that hard work pays off in the long run. Thank you for sharing your wisdom with us. You truly are the best.

To Ariane Laezza—you always manage to achieve the impossible in the most effortless way. Thank you for contributing your visual talents and professional insights. There's no one's eye we trust more with our work.

To Chef Christine Flynn—thank you for always telling it like it is. We respect you so hard, and we thank our lucky stars that our paths crossed at the (now infamous) iQ Food Co. launch in 2018.

To Lisa Corbo, a.k.a. Fashion Mom—*grazie, bella*, for your perspective, your way of life, your fearlessness, and your undeniably bold character. You showed us the way of the rebel exactly when we needed to learn it, and you inspire us to keep evolving always.

To Sarah Thompson, possibly the best thing to have sprung forth from the awesomeness that is the Rebel Mama's private Facebook group—you are a voice of reason in an unreasonable world. You also happen to be one hell of a lawyer. Thank you for empowering us with your legal prowess.

To Dr. Andrea Gelinas, a.k.a. Beluch—it was love at first sight. Thank you for being a solid friend, an interior design renegade, a great storyteller, and the best damn dentist a gal could ever ask for.

To Jacqui Wilkins—thank you for agreeing to our last-minute request to be interviewed and providing academically inclined mamas with exactly the kind of insight and inspiration they need.

To Mariana Iordanova, a.k.a. the Wolf—thanks for sending us *all of the* real estate suggestions so our readers could squeeze the most out of their properties and drive those values up. We'll be sure to invite you to our future infinity pool party (or you can invite us to yours).

To José—thank you for not only lending your beautiful flowchart-making talents to this book but also being the best tequila partner in crime.

To Ashley—for jumping on the opportunity and lending your solid design skills to this book.

To Alessandra—you fact-checked all the accounting information we spewed with a tiny human on your boob. You're a hero. Thank you.

To Abby—thank you for helping us help moms land their dream jobs (s/o to my sister for bringing us together).

To strong Italian coffee—thank you for helping us get through compound interest, managing debt, tax sheltering, and all the other buzzkills that come with financial literacy. Seriously, the research almost made us keel over and die. Good thing we're insured now.

To weed—for helping us conjure up unexpected and clever ways to ensure that this money book was not like all the rest (boring). The "hot guy/girl breaks" are all you, and we're pretty sure everyone's here for that.

Speaking of hot guy/girl breaks, thank you to Michael Steele and Ariane Laezza for gracing these pages with your whimsical charm and effortless sexy.

To HarperCollins—you understood who we are and what we need from our very first meeting. Thank you for being a dream publisher to work with, for giving us the literary space to extend our voice, and for agreeing that profanity is simply necessary sometimes.

Finally, we'd like to take this opportunity to acknowledge our various privileges—namely race, colour, ability, sexual orientation, and class—the very things that allowed us access to the knowledge, information, and insider tips that are now bound in the pages of this book. We hope it has left you inspired not only to learn, but to share your findings with others. Use that privilege wisely, girl.

CREATIVE
CONTRIBUTORS

This page and the Notes section that follows constitute a continuation of the copyright page.

Photographs on pages viii–ix, xviii–xix, 28, 38, 43, 56, 66, 68, 75, 90–91, 128, 130, 171, 180, 182, 194–95, 202 © 2020 by Ariane Laezza.

Illustrations on pages xx, 98 © 2020 by Ashley Tse.

Text on page 34 by Dr. Andrea Gelinas.

Text on page 92 by Lisa Corbo.

Text on pages 150 and 168 by Christine Flynn.

Oh yeah, and us. We threw a couple of photos in here, too.

Photographs and illustrations on pages vii, 2, 8, 10, 11, 22, 64, 80, 106, 118, 120, 134, 140, 154, 158, 162, 167, 175, 187, 191, 192, courtesy of Aleksandra Jassem.

Photograph on page 48 from the collection of Nikita Stanley.

Styling on pages viii–ix, 38, 43, 56, 75, 128, 171, 182 by Nikita Stanley.

Styling on pages xviii–xix, 28, 66, 90, 91, 202 by Lisa Corbo.

NOTES

The Price of Motherhood

In "The Price of Motherhood," we relied on many sources to paint a picture of gendered financial inequities. These included the following:

Maggie McGrath's *Forbes* magazine article "Why Being a Woman Can Cost You More Than $400,000" (April 5, 2006): https://www.forbes.com/sites/maggiemcgrath/2016/04/05/why-being-a-woman-can-cost-you-more-than-400000.

Brittany Lambert and Kate McInturff's "Making Women Count: The Unequal Economics of Women's Work," Oxfam Canada and the Canadian Centre for Policy Alternatives (2016): https://www.policyalternatives.ca/sites/default/files/uploads/publications/National%20Office/2016/03/Making_Women_Count2016.pdf.

Lauren Smith Brody's Wealthsimple article "How to Avoid the Mom Penalty" (June 16, 2019): https://www.wealthsimple.com/en-ca/magazine/how-to-avoid-the-mom-penalty.

Gaëlle Ferrant, Luca Maria Pesando, and Keiko Nowacka's study "Unpaid Care Work: The Missing Link in the Analysis of Gender Gaps in Labour Outcomes," OECD Development Centre (December 2014): https://www.oecd.org/dev/development-gender/Unpaid_care_work.pdf.

Michelle Fox's CNBC article "The 'Motherhood Penalty' Is Real, and It Costs Women $16,000 a Year in Lost Wages" (March 25, 2019): https://www.cnbc.com/2019/03/25/the-motherhood-penalty-costs-women-16000-a-year-in-lost-wages.html.

Lisa Miller's Wealthsimple article "Marriage: The Money Story" (March 7, 2019): https://www.wealthsimple.com/en-ca/magazine/marriage-money-story.

Marianne Bertrand, Emir Kamenica, and Jessica Pan's study, "Gender Identity and Relative Income Within Households," *Quarterly Journal of Economics* (2015), 571–614: https://faculty.chicagobooth.edu/emir.kamenica/documents/identity.pdf.

Part 1: Planning
How Much Do Kids Actually Cost?

To answer this question with the dismaying facts, we turned to Barry Choi's *Financial Post* article "What Does It Cost to Raise a Child in Canada?" (May 19, 2020): https://financialpost.com/moneywise/what-does-it-cost-to-raise-a-child-in-canada.

The Cost of Raising a Child calculator can be found at this website: https://themeasureofaplan.com/cost-of-raising-a-child-calculator/.

Joining Finances

The first section of this chapter is adapted, with permission, from the Wealthsimple article "How to Open a Joint Account without All the Resentment (or Bankruptcy)" (August 18, 2017): https://www.wealthsimple.com/en-ca/magazine/how-to-joint-account.

"Structuring a Joint Account" takes inspiration from the suggestions in LearnVest's article for *Forbes* magazine "How to Combine Finances with Your Partner" (September 10, 2012): https://www.forbes.com/sites/learnvest/2012/09/10/how-to-combine-finances-with-your-partner. We also reference Dennis Hammer's Wealthsimple article "How to Follow the 50/30/20 Rule" (September 25, 2019): https://www.wealthsimple.com/en-ca/learn/50-30-20-rule.

Wills, Guardianship, and Other Morbid Thoughts

This chapter is adapted, with permission, from the Wealthsimple article "Everything You Need to Know About Drafting a Will" (July 25, 2016): https://www.wealthsimple.com/en-ca/magazine/how-to-draft-a-will.

Life Insurance (Yawn)

This chapter is adapted, with permission, from the Wealthsimple article "A Totally-Not-Boring Guide to Life Insurance" (September 12, 2017): https://www.wealthsimple.com/en-ca/magazine/how-to-life-insurance. For more about the marijuana policy update, read Pete Evans's article for CBC News "Life Insurance Companies No Longer Treating Marijuana Use as High Risk as Tobacco" (July 2, 2018): https://www.cbc.ca/news/business/marijuana-life-insurance-1.4722763.

What About Lone Parents?

The Canadian statistics provided in the first paragraph (and regarding the average monthly and annual income for solo moms) come from Statistics Canada's "Lone-Parent Families," Insights on Canadian Society (November 27, 2015): https://www150.statcan .gc.ca/n1/pub/75-006-x/2015001/article/14202/parent-eng.htm. The global data in this paragraph comes from page 6 of the United Nation's booklet "Household Size and Composition Around the World 2017": https://www.un.org/en/development/desa /population/publications/pdf/ageing/household_size_and_composition_around_the _world_2017_data_booklet.pdf.

For the 2018 average male annual income, we consulted Statistics Canada's Table 11-10-0239-01, "Income of Individuals by Age Group, Sex and Income Source, Canada, Provinces and Selected Census Metropolitan Areas": https://doi.org/10.25318/1110023901-eng.

For further information about the Employment Insurance Family Supplement, visit https://www.canada.ca/en/employment-social-development/programs/ei/ei-list /reports/regular-benefits/situations.html#h2.3.

Our source for information about the Child Rearing provision was Jim Yih's article "Child rearing drop out—parents can get more out of CPP," *RetireHappy* (December 19, 2019): https://retirehappy.ca/child-rearing-drop-out-parents-can-get/. Details about US tax breaks like the Earned Income Tax Credit and the Child Tax Credit can be found here: https://www.irs.gov/credits-deductions/individuals/earned-income-tax-credit and https://www.taxpolicycenter.org/briefing-book/what-child-tax-credit.

Part 2: Earning
The Bo$$

Most of the "Parental Leave" section is adapted, with permission, from the Wealthsimple article "How to Afford to Take the Parental Leave You Want" (July 3, 2017): https:// www.wealthsimple.com/en-ca/magazine/how-to-parental-leave. For details about Canada's 18-month-leave option, please see: https://www.canada.ca/en/services /benefits/ei/ei-maternity-parental.html.

The section "10 Reasons Why Dad Should Definitely Take Parental Leave" is adapted, with permission, from Lauren Smith Brody's Wealthsimple article "How to Avoid the

Mom Penalty" (June 16, 2019): https://www.wealthsimple.com/en-ca/magazine
/how-to-avoid-the-mom-penalty.

The quoted and paraphrased material from Jared Cline are from "10 Reasons Every
Company Should Offer Paid Paternity Leave (and Every Father Should Take It),"
Catalyst: Workplaces That Work for Women (June 12, 2019): https://www.catalyst
.org/2019/06/12/10-reasons-every-company-should-offer-paid-paternity-leave-and
-every-father-should-take-it/.

Elly-Ann Johansson shares her findings in "The Effect of Own and Spousal Parental
Leave on Earnings," Working Paper for the Institute for Labour Market Policy Evaluation
(March 22, 2010), and the quote we've included is from page 28: https://core.ac.uk
/reader/6352598.

In "Resuming an Old Job as a New Woman, " the section "Advocating for Yourself at
Work" is adapted, with permission, from Lauren Smith Brody's Wealthsimple article
"How to Avoid the Mom Penalty" (June 16 2019): https://www.wealthsimple.com
/en-ca/magazine/how-to-avoid-the-mom-penalty.

The Rebel Mama Resumé in "Building Your Resumé (from the Ground Up)" first
appeared on pages 50–51 of our previous book, *The Rebel Mama Handbook (for Cool Moms)*.

For tips for seeing the mat leave gap as an advantage, check out Addie Swartz's LinkedIn
article "Gaps in the Resumé, But Not in Talent—Reasons to Embrace Women Returning
to the Workforce" (August 3, 2017): https://business.linkedin.com/talent-solutions/blog
/op-ed/2017/gaps-in-the-resume-but-not-in-talent-reasons-to-embrace-women
-returning-to-the-workforce.

For the tips found in "Your Best Job Interview Ever in 10 Steps," we looked to Indeed.
com's article " How to Prepare for an Interview" (May 29, 2020): https://www.indeed
.com/career-advice/interviewing/how-to-prepare-for-an-interview.

The Hu$tler

In "Exploring Entrepreneurship," data on the failure rate for new Canadian start-ups came
from the government's report "Canadian New Firms: Birth and Survival Rates over the
Period 2002–2014, May 2018": https://www.ic.gc.ca/eic/site/061.nsf/eng/h_03075.html.

The $cholar

For more information about the options outlined in "Academic Loans and Grants," visit www.canlearn.ca and https://www.canada.ca/en/services/benefits/education/student -aid/grants-loans.

For more information about apprenticeships, visit https://www.canada.ca/en /employment-social-development/services/apprentices/become-apprentice.html and www.red-seal.ca.

The $AHM

In "Imposter Syndrome (and How to Avoid Falling Victim to It)," we drew on the following resources:

Rachel Sharp writes about gender differences and imposter syndrome in "Two-Thirds of Women Experience Imposter Syndrome," *HR Magazine* (July 31, 2018): https://www .hrmagazine.co.uk/article-details/two-thirds-of-women-experience-imposter-syndrome.

Melody Wilding gives an overview of insights from Dr. Valerie Young's book, *The Secret Thoughts of Successful Women: Why Capable People Suffer from the Imposter Syndrome and How to Thrive in Spite of It* in her article "The Five Types of Impostor Syndrome and How to Beat Them," Fast Company (May 18, 2017): https://www.fastcompany.com/40421352 /the-five-types-of-impostor-syndrome-and-how-to-beat-them.

For the data in the third paragraph of "Making It Work, Equitably," we drew on the following two sources: Eileen Patten's article "How American Parents Balance Work and Family Life When Both Work," Pew Research Center (November 4, 2015): https://www .pewresearch.org/fact-tank/2015/11/04/how-american-parents-balance-work-and -family-life-when-both-work/; and Jessica Valenti's "Kids Don't Damage Women's Careers—Men Do," *Medium* (September 13, 2018): https://gen.medium.com /kids-dont-damage-women-s-careers-men-do-eb07cba689b8.

One study that links creative activities to better job performance was conducted by Kevin Eschleman, Jamie Madsen, Gene Alarcon, and Alex Barelka, and published as "Benefiting from Creative Activity: The Positive Relationships Between Creative Activity, Recovery Experiences, and Performance-Related Outcomes," in the *Journal of Occupational and*

Organizational Psychology (April 17, 2014). It's summarized in SF State News: https://news
.sfsu.edu/creative-activities-outside-work-can-improve-job-performance.

Part 3: Spending
Childcare Expenses (Read 'em and Weep)

For data about Canadian daycare fees, we're indebted to David Macdonald and Martha
Friendly's study "Time Out: Child Care Fees in Canada 2017," Canadian Centre for
Policy Alternatives (December 2017): https://www.policyalternatives.ca/sites/default
/files/uploads/publications/National%20Office/2017/12/Time%20Out.pdf. The first
block quote in the "Daycare" section is from page 4 of this study; the costs of toddler and
preschool care in Toronto are found on pages 11 and 13 respectively; and rural southwestern Ontario fees appear on page 17.

For information about nanny wages, we drew on data collected by Canadiannanny.ca,
which is presented in their blog post "How Much Does a Nanny Cost" (September 14,
2018): https://canadiannanny.ca/how-much-does-a-nanny-cost. For a closer look at the
benefits and drawbacks of nanny sharing, as well as tips on how to make it work for your
family, check out Martha Scully's blog post "Nanny Sharing: Pros, Cons, & How-To"
(April 11, 2017): https://canadiannanny.ca/nanny-sharing-in-canada.

We drew on the following resources for details about hosting an au pair: https://
aupaircanada.net/en_US/host-family-in-canada-costs-and-working-hours-of-au-pairs/
and https://aupaircanada.net/en_US/fees/.

Part 4: Debt
Step One: Find Out Your Credit Score and Step Two: Improve Your Credit Score

These chapters are adapted, with permission, from Andrew Goldman's Wealthsimple
article "What's a Good Credit Score?" (July 31, 2018): https://www.wealthsimple.com
/en-ca/learn/good-credit-score and Danielle Kubes's Wealthsimple article "How to
Improve Your Credit Score" (December 1, 2019): https://www.wealthsimple.com/en-ca
/learn/how-to-improve-credit-score.

Step Three: Figure Out Your Debt-to-Income Ratio

This chapter is adapted, with permission, from Dennis Hammer's Wealthsimple article
"Debt to Income Ratio Explained" (last updated August 28, 2019): https://www
.wealthsimple.com/en-ca/learn/debt-to-income-ratio.

Step Four: Improve Your Debt-to-Income Ratio

For information about the debt snowball and debt avalanche strategies for paying off debt, we consulted the following resources: Dave Ramsey's blog post "How to Get Out of Debt with the Debt Snowball Plan": https://www.daveramsey.com/blog/get-out-of-debt-with -the-debt-snowball-plan and Jamie Friedlander's post "Debt Avalanche vs. Debt Snowball: Which Payoff Method Is Right for You?" MagnifyMoney (November 14, 2018): https://www.magnifymoney.com/blog/pay-down-my-debt/debt-avalanche-vs-debt -snowball/#Howdoesthedebtavalanchemethodwork.

The "Pro Tips" at the end of "Step Four" are adapted, with permission, from Dennis Hammer's Wealthsimple article "Debt to Income Ratio Explained" (last updated August 28, 2019): https://www.wealthsimple.com/en-ca/learn/debt-to-income-ratio.

Household Investments

The table "What's Worth Doing in Your Home" is adapted, with permission, from the Wealthsimple article "How to Make Home Improvements That Are Also Good Investments" (August 3, 2017): https://www.wealthsimple.com/en-ca/magazine/how-to -home-improvement.

Part 5: Saving

Budgeting (Phase Two)

The section "The 50/30/20 Rule" is adapted, with permission, from Dennis Hammer's Wealthsimple article "How to Follow the 50/30/20 Rule" (September 25, 2019): https:// www.wealthsimple.com/en-ca/learn/50-30-20-rule.

Food for Thought (Less Waste and More Money in Your Pocket)

The data about Canadian household spending on groceries comes from Erica Alini's article for Global News "How Much Does a Week of Groceries Cost in Canada? We Crunched the Numbers" (November 7, 2017): https://globalnews.ca/news/3828492/healthy-food -cost-canada/. To find out how much food the average Canadian consumer wastes, we consulted the following transcript of an episode of CBC's *The Current*, "How Bad is Canada's Food Waste Problem? Among the World's Worst, Report Finds" (April 5, 2018): https:// www.cbc.ca/radio/thecurrent/the-current-for-april-5-2018-1.4605392/how-bad-is-canada -s-food-waste-problem-among-the-world-s-worst-report-finds-1.4606012.

For food shopping and saving tips, we drew on "12 Ways to Save Big on Groceries and Shop on a Budget," MyMoneyCoach: https://www.mymoneycoach.ca/saving-money /saving-on-groceries.

Compound Interest (Your BFF)

This chapter is adapted, with permission, from Andrew Goldman and Luisa Rollenhagen's Wealthsimple article "What Is Compound Interest?" (last updated May 22, 2020): https://www.wealthsimple.com/en-ca/learn/what-is-compound-interest.

Tax Sheltering 101

The section "Registered Retirement Savings Plan (RRSP)" is adapted, with permission, from Andrew Goldman's Wealthsimple article "What Is an RRSP and How Does It Work?" (last updated March 3, 2020): https://www.wealthsimple.com/en-ca/learn /what-is-rrsp. Further details about the RRSP Home Buyers' Plan are drawn from the Government of Canada website "How to Withdraw Funds from RRSP(s) Under the Home Buyers' Plan (HBP)": https://www.canada.ca/en/revenue-agency/services/tax /individuals/topics/rrsps-related-plans/what-home-buyers-plan/withdraw-funds -rrsp-s-under-home-buyers-plan.html.

The section "Tax-Free Savings Account (TFSA)" is adapted, with permission, from Andrew Goldman's Wealthsimple article "Tax Free Savings Account (TFSA)" (last updated June 18, 2020): https://www.wealthsimple.com/en-ca/learn/what-is-tfsa.

The section "Registered Education Savings Plan (RESP)" is adapted, with permission, from Andrew Goldman and Luisa Rollenhagen's Wealthsimple article "What's an RESP (Registered Education Savings Plan) and How It Works" (last updated June 3, 2020): https://www.wealthsimple.com/en-ca/learn/what-is-resp.

Part 6: Investing
Investing 101

In "Assets and Liabilities," we paraphrased Robert T. Kiyosaki's observations on the subject from his book *Rich Dad Poor Dad: What the Rich Teach Their Kids About Money That the Poor and Middle Class Do Not!* (Plata Publishing: 2017), 197.

The section "Investment Options" is adapted, with permission, from the following Wealthsimple articles:

Danielle Kubes's "What Is a GIC 1500?" (August 28, 2019): https://www.wealthsimple.com/en-ca/learn/what-is-gic.

Dennis Hammer's "Types of Bonds Explained" (May 14, 2020): https://www.wealthsimple.com/en-ca/learn/types-of-bonds-explained.

Luisa Rollenhagen's and Andrew Goldman's "What Are Mutual Funds? And How to Invest in Them" (June 30, 2020): https://www.wealthsimple.com/en-ca/learn/how-to-invest-in-mutual-funds.

Andrew Goldman's "What's an ETF—The Ultimate Guide" (September 18, 2019): https://www.wealthsimple.com/en-us/learn/what-is-etf.

For the information about stocks, we consulted Kimberly Amadeo's "What Are Stocks?" *The Balance* (January 22, 2020): https://www.thebalance.com/what-are-stocks-3306181.